Scripture and Discernment

SCRIPTURE & DISCERNMENT
Decision Making In The Church

LUKE TIMOTHY JOHNSON

Abingdon Press
Nashville

SCRIPTURE AND DISCERNMENT: DECISION MAKING IN THE CHURCH

Copyright © 1983 assigned to Luke Timothy Johnson

New text and revisions copyright © 1996 Abingdon Press

This book is printed on acid-free, recycled paper.

Library of Congress Cataloging-in-Publication Data

Johnson, Luke Timothy.
  Scripture and discernment: decision-making in the church / Luke
Timothy Johnson.
    p.   cm.
  Expanded and revised version of Decision making in the church : a
biblical model. c1982
  Includes bibliographical references.
  ISBN 0-687-01238-4 (pbk.: alk. paper)
    1. Decision-making, Group—Religious aspects—Christianity.
2. Decision-making, Group, in the Bible.   3. Bible. N.T. Acts X-
XV—Criticism, interpretation, etc.   I. Title.
BV652.2.J65   1996
262—dc20   95-50579
                                                                        CIP
ISBN 13: 978-0-687-01238-1

Scripture quotations are the author's own translation, or are from the Revised Standard Version of the Bible, copyright 1946, 1952, 1971 by the Division of Christian Education of the National Council of the Churches of Christ in the USA. Used by permission.

An adaptation of "The Authority of the New Testament in the Church," in Charles R. Blaisdell, ed., *Conservative, Moderate, Liberal: The Biblical Authority Debate* (St. Louis: CBP Press, 1991), pp. 87-99, appears on pp. 36-46. Reprinted by permission of Chalice Press.

An adaptation of "Debate and Discernment: Scripture and the Spirit," *Commonweal* 121/2 (January 28, 1994): 11-13, appears on pp. 144-48.

An adaptation of "Discerning God's Word," *Priests & People* 9 (1995): 137-40 appears on pp. 155-58.

08 09 10 11 12 13 14 15 — 18 17 16 15 14 13 12 11

MANUFACTURED IN THE UNITED STATES OF AMERICA

CONTENTS

PREFACE

This book tries to place the decision-making process of the church within a biblical and theological framework. An earlier version of it called *Decision Making in the Church: A Biblical Model* was published by Fortress Press in 1982. Possibly because it fell between the cracks of publishing convention, it received only one serious review and quickly went out of print. Yet, it stubbornly refused to disappear altogether. Some students of Luke-Acts found its reading of Acts 10–15 helpful. Some theologians found that it provided an example of "narrative theology." Most significant, some people active in parish ministry found its ideas provocative even if hard to put into practice. So, small numbers of copies continued to circulate and be used long after the book went out of print.

At the same time, I had kept working at some of the ideas that I first expressed here. In *Faith's Freedom: A Classic Spirituality for Contemporary Christians* (Minneapolis: Fortress Press, 1990), I attempted a "reading" of the Christian life along the lines I had earlier suggested. And in other contexts, I wrote articles and gave lectures devoted to my understanding of theology as the discernment of God's Word.

The sense that the original book might still prove useful to the church and that my additional essays might also increase the value of its proposals by clarifying, expanding, and contextualizing them, encouraged Rex Matthews of Abingdon Press to proceed with this second, expanded edition under the appropriately fuller title, *Scripture and Discernment: Decision Making in the Church*. Some parts of the original book remain intact. Others have been elaborated. And the book has been expanded by the addition of new sections. I hope that the overall line of argument remains clean and if anything more convincing.

A considerable amount of the exegetical material was first prepared for the Luke-Acts task force of the Catholic Biblical Association in two papers: "The Use of Acts 15 in the Theology of the Church: A Scouting Report" (1978), and "The Church Reaching Decision: A Theological Reading of Acts

10–15" (1979). The constructive responses of Bill Kurz, Dennis Hamm, and Rea McDonnell were encouraging. In the summer of 1978 many of the ideas of chapter 1 were developed in three lectures given to the East Ohio Methodist Conference College of Preachers, under the rubric "The Pastor as Theologian." David Wilcox enabled and encouraged this venture. I have since had the pleasure of having Bishop James S. Thomas, who was my host at that conference, become my colleague at Candler School of Theology. Some other ideas were worked through at a Yale-Warner Memorial Presbyterian Church symposium held in Kensington, Maryland, in 1982. David Graybill and Carol Strickland provided David Kelsey and me opportunity to spend time thinking about these issues. The benefit to my own thought of Kelsey's conversation and writing outweighs, I hope, any damage I have done to his.

Other parts of this book began life elsewhere: The discussion of the authority of the New Testament in the church was first a lecture at a conference at Christian Theological Seminary in Indianapolis sponsored by the Lilly Foundation, and appeared in *Conservative, Moderate, Liberal: The Biblical Theology Debate*, edited by Charles R. Blaisdell (St. Louis: CPB Press, 1990), pp. 87-99. The article entitled "Fragments of an Untidy Conversation: Theology and the Literary Diversity of the New Testament" appeared in a *Festschrift* for Christiaan Beker edited by Steven Kraftchick and Ben Ollenburger, *Biblical Theology: Problems and Perspectives* (Nashville: Abingdon Press, 1995). Some of the ideas on homosexuality were worked out in an article called "Debate and Discernment: Scripture and the Spirit," *Commonweal* 121 (1994): 11-13. The material on edification and holiness as criteria for discernment was developed for Convocation Lectures at Eden Theological Seminary in 1992 and refined in the William Porcher Dubose Lectures at Sewanee School of Theology in 1995. The section on preaching was published as an article, "Preaching as the Discernment of God's Word," for *Priests and People* 9 (1995): 137-40.

My particular thanks to all those who have invited me to speak over the years when I was trying to think these things through, to Bob Ratcliff of Abingdon Press for his help in stitching the materials together into a reasonably coherent manuscript, and to all my students from Yale Divinity School, Indiana University, and now Emory University, who have shared so many narratives of faith with me over the past twenty years, who showed me that the ideas work when they are tried, and who cheered for Peter and Paul and James when they heard what they had done. This book is dedicated to them, for without them, there would have been nothing to write.

Luke Timothy Johnson
Atlanta, Georgia, 1995

INTRODUCTION

I invite you in this book to an exercise in practical theology. Practical thinking is messy. Most of us are strong on theory, for theory is clear and clean and stands still. But thinking about the ever-shifting face of real life brings terror to the mind. The subject matter does not hold steady. Worse, it takes hold of the thinker, preventing distance and discretion. These qualities are admired before all others in science, so practical thinking is sometimes considered less serious than the sort given to molecules and mollusks. It is not, of course. It only requires quicker feet.

The subject of reaching decision in the church is just such a practical topic in both the loose and strict sense. It is practical in the sense that it is "useful," because it is something done by people in the church all the time. Some thinking about it might be pertinent. It is also practical in the strict sense: It has to do, not with theory, but with practice (praxis). What the church does when it makes decisions concerns us here.

The subject matter is so common, however, and so deceptively available, that it is necessary to back up a little and make clear what aspect of it demands attention and why. Otherwise, we might get lost. We might discover that some fundamental presupposition, which we thought we shared, suddenly divides us and keeps us from moving farther. You might, for example, have something different in your mind when you say "church" than I do. Likewise, your understanding of "faith" and "theology" could well be far distant from my own. However practical the goal of this book, then, it inevitably involves some theory. This should not surprise. Practical issues have a way of cracking open the world of our presuppositions, and demanding of us a reexamination of our most basic perceptions.

This is certainly not a sociological analysis, with graphs and charts showing how dioceses and denominations reach decisions. The way groups act when they make decisions, however, is of considerable interest to our discussion. Nor is this a strictly historical study, although some documents from the past will demand more than passing attention. And even though I do make some suggestions about making decisions, this is not really a manual of instructions. I want to think with you about the way decision making in the church can be a theological process, and how that way of thinking about it can make a difference for specific ecclesial communities.

What you will find here, then, is a kind of theological reflection on the nuts and bolts of the church's life. I have a bias. I think there ought to be some connection between what a group claims to be, and the way it does things. The church claims to be a community of faith; is there any connection between this claim and its actual communal life? This could be tested by looking at several places where churches express their life, but a particularly important and revealing place is the process of reaching decision.

I must admit to another bias, this one perhaps disproportionately important in my thinking on this issue. This bias says that when the church makes decisions, the Bible ought somehow to be involved. This is a strong but not terribly helpful bias, for it raises more problems than it settles. How should the Bible be involved? Specters of proof-texting float before our anxious eyes. If such shadows are to be dispersed, we must come to grips with the legitimate and necessary connections between the use of Scripture in theology, the place of theology in the church, and the contribution made by both to that process by which the church discerns and decides its identity in the present for the future. Even though the language sounds slightly pretentious, this book uses an aspect of practical church life as a way of thinking about ecclesial hermeneutics.

The book falls into three sections. Part 1 is more explicitly theoretical, seeking first to establish some working definitions, and then engaging some debated questions concerning the role of Scripture. Part 2 is textual and exegetical: I consider the difficulties facing the use of the New Testament on the issue of decision making, analyze the texts that are most useful (especially Acts 10–15), and then develop the key notion of discernment through a reading of Paul. Part 3 is practical. I first discuss three kinds of decisions facing churches: leadership, fellowship, and stewardship. Then I suggest two kinds of pastoral devices for creating communities of discernment within which decision making as a theological process might take place.

PART ONE

THEORY

CHAPTER 1

DEFINITIONS

I call this first set of remarks "theoretical," not because they are particularly abstract, but because they provide the presuppositions and perspectives I bring to the subject of decision making. Conversations are too often derailed by inattention to such simple matters as the definition of terms. I begin, then, with my definitions of the terms I will be using. They are not necessarily anybody else's definitions, but they are the ones that operate in this book.

Our interest is in the process of reaching decision by the social group called the church. What do I mean by "decision"? Nothing more complicated than the choice undertaken by a group to act in one way rather than another. The fascinating but distracting issue of *individual* decision making must resolutely be left aside, except as it may pertain to the life of the group. Whether decisions are ever actually made is something else we cannot prove but only assert. Talk about decisions implies that people are free to choose. Some philosophers deny that this happens. Since human freedom is illusory, they say, so also is the apparent freedom found in decisions. Choices can always be reduced to biological, psychological, and social forces. Neither the partial truth of this position nor its attractiveness need be denied. Much of the human enterprise is undoubtedly determined by the factors so minutely scrutinized by the detractors of this freedom.

Even if it is foolish, however, to deny that multiple factors determine human choice, there is a hint of madness in the opinion that says choices are never free. The madness lies in equating reality with our ways of analyzing it. When we look at choices after the fact we can always find their causes. Hindsight reduces freedom to fate. Yet freedom is experienced in the act itself, even by those who deny it in their studies. In fact, the denial of freedom by one fated to hold that view is not worth much consideration. The notion of freedom appears to be, like the concept of God, necessary for its own effective rebuttal.

Thus, I will assume here that freedom is real and often a factor in the decisions made by individuals and groups, even though the forces of determination should also be given their due, for not every decision is so freely made as it appears to be. For example, both congressional votes and political platitudes often have a certain admirable predictability, yet occasionally even politicians surprise.

DECISION MAKING IN GROUPS

Some group decisions are stimulated by the choices made by individual members of the group. Sometimes the group as such is required to act because of the frequency and vigor of individual actions threatening the group's identity. Such is the case with deviance in behavior and heresy in doctrine. Groups have a fragile hold on their existence. They depend on the commitment of their members to the way things are done, and the reasons for so doing them. Groups have, therefore, only limited tolerance for diversity. When that tolerance is overstepped, the group will either dissolve or make decisions. Even apart from the challenges posed by the choices made by individuals, groups must make decisions for the body as a whole. No matter how small or large the group, whether it be family, club, school, city, state, or nation; as soon as the pronoun is "we" rather than "I," a group's decision-making mechanisms are invoked.

All groups make both *task* decisions and *identity* decisions. The distinction is a loose one, with disputed borders. Task decisions tend to raise identity issues, and identity decisions require expression by specific tasks. Still, the distinction has some validity. Task decisions concern the functions to be performed by the group, whether of the maintenance and upkeep variety ("How can we keep the machine going?"), or of the missions and vocation variety ("What does this machine make, anyway?").

When groups are defined by a single task, they find that identity and task decisions are almost identical, and relatively easier to make. A group whose sole reason for existing is to explore caves would do well to have an expert spelunker at its head, and if it were transported to the Sahara Desert, would need to reconsider its future as a group. A "task force" appointed to study an economic problem has only that for its goal, and should care little about its members' lives apart from their expertise and ability to work together.

Identity decisions are also required of all groups. Membership questions fall into this category: Who can be admitted to the group, and under what conditions? Decisions on boundaries also implicate the identity of the group: How can we define, symbolize, and keep effective the lines between "us" and "them"? A third type of identity question deals with discipline and correction within the group: How do we measure failure and success? How is one punished and the other rewarded? What constitutes deviance, and at what point can we no longer tolerate deviance? What does it mean when a member of the group is expelled? Decisions of this sort are made less on the basis of efficiency, as should be the case with task decisions, than on the basis of self-understanding. When decisions must be made concerning leadership and its rights and responsibilities, both task and identity questions are involved.

The distinctions obviously oversimplify complex processes, but some groups tend to be defined more by the tasks they perform, while others by simply "being" a certain way. It is not always possible to distinguish one from the other since both kinds of groups make both task and identity decisions. Nevertheless, it is fair to say that groups defined by "being" a certain way (a "community of the pure," a "witness to the truth," a "school of the Lord's service") will find decisions concerning "identity" more difficult and threatening than those concerning tasks. For groups whose purpose is fulfilled by a certain kind of "doing," on the other hand, "task" decisions will be more difficult.

In making decisions of any sort, a group reveals itself as a group, and it does this by becoming itself as a group. Decision making is a fundamental articulation of a group's life. The process by which decision is reached tells of the nature of the group in a way other forms of ritual sometimes miss. Perhaps a community loudly proclaims its democratic lifestyle—and at work, rest, and meals, the members hold all things equally. But if the community's decisions are made by executive decree, the claim to equality is empty; the group actually has an authoritarian structure. Conversely, if decisions on entrance and advancement, leadership and responsibility are made by a genuinely popular vote, that process reveals the group to be democratic in a way that propaganda never could.

Qualifications for taking part in the decision-making process also tell us a great deal about the nature of the group. Property, gender, or age qualifications for voting give specific shading to the kind of democracy this is. The fact that we vote to make decisions tells us that we are a democracy. The fact that not all of us who are members of the group can vote tells us that this democracy is not absolute but relative. If it is possible for a member to lose a vote, that tells us how seriously we take responsibility or deviance. And if members of a group have the vote but do not use it, we learn of a profound alienation of the members from the life of the group.

The decision-making process in groups may be camouflaged, so that it takes effort to discover the genuine structure of the group. In complex social organisms, the apparent and hidden functions of structures frequently become mixed. In a large university, for example, the faculty may be convinced that it decides the direction of the school through its committees which debate and decide policy issues. But faculty meetings and committees often better serve the hidden functions of socialization and energy diffusion than the apparent function of governance. Meanwhile, a poorly legitimated but effective bureaucracy does the real steering. The fact that processes can be counterfeited and hard to detect, however, does not deny their power to reveal the group's nature when finally found. A university run by administrators rather than faculty may be an admirable society, but its decisions are likely to be made on the basis of financial or political considerations rather than strictly academic ones. To that extent, it may no longer be the kind of group its members still conceive it to be.

Groups, and the myths which legitimate them, are conservative by nature and resistant to change. It requires considerable energy for individuals simply to maintain, much less challenge, their social world. Many group decisions, as a result, tend to be made implicitly, following the path of least resistance. This is the path of "what we have always done."

In the absence of challenge from without, for example, the process of admission to the group will never change. Practice is reinforced by precedent. If only adult males have applied for membership in the past, then only adult males will have been admitted. The force of this precedent will make the admission of anyone else a major adjustment. Along with the practice, the perceptions of the group become petrified. The continued admission of only adult males begins to suggest that this is a "males only" group. Structure reinforces ideology. If we are asked why we admit only males, we shall probably find reasons why ours is the sort of group in which only males can participate.

Practices become *explicit* in their structure and ideology when challenged by the possibility of change. It is only when adult women seek admission to our group that our previous habits and presuppositions will be called into question. The challenge to change forces a decision.

Now the members must find reasons why women should or should not be admitted.

Let us imagine that our hypothetical group is called "Scientists United." Now we must decide whether, in spite of our title, we have been all along simply a "male support group" (and can therefore legitimately exclude women), or have genuinely been a "scientific association" (which can find no reason for excluding women scientists). Whichever way the decision goes, the process of reaching it will show us the true identity of the group. The decision, furthermore, will give more definite shape to the group's identity than it had in earlier, innocent, and unchallenged times.

The threat of change forces a group to make its previously implicit choices explicit. In the process, it must identify both the challenge and its own nature as a group. The identification process is reciprocal. The challenge is perceived in terms of the group's previous understanding, but in turn, it calls to the surface aspects of that understanding which had been latent. Making decisions, then, always involves a process of interpretation. Even when carried out after the fact, such interpretation tries to get at the question, "Why did we do that?" and will likely answer it, "Because we are that kind of group." Once accustomed ways are called into question, both the voice of change and the voice of tradition require interpretation.

The demand for group interpretation raises other questions about the dynamics of decision making. Who in the group is responsible for carrying out this interpretation? Is the task entrusted to one person? If so, on what basis? Or are others involved in the interpretation? If so, how do they express their understanding? Do they interpret by their vote alone, or do they give voice to their understanding in any other way? And whose voices are listened to? Are those seeking membership, for example, included in the process? Are they interviewed to discover their reasons for seeking entrance? Or does such a hearing prejudice the issue by already inserting them into the decision-making process?

Other questions concern the norms by which the group interprets itself and makes decisions. The demand for decision challenges a group's identity and requires its interpretation. But where is the measure for this identity? Does our group have a constitution with bylaws? Do we operate on the basis of a collection of precedents? Do we find the measure for our identity in the body of stories and customs which forms our tradition? Do we have a "founding document" we regard as authoritative?

Finding the normative expression of the group's identity only begins the interpretative process, for we must consider what role those norms will play when confronted by the pressure of the present situation and the current mood of the members. To state that the charter is normative does not yet say how it will be normative. Perhaps it does not appear to address the present circumstances at all, or addresses them only ambiguously. How much weight will be given to tradition and how much to present experience, and who will do the weighing? The answers to these questions, too, tell us much about the nature of the group.

The dilemma of the group called "Scientists United" is simple enough to let me summarize the observations I have been making and suggestive enough to point toward the same process in the church. We remember that the group had only male members until women asked to join. Now what must we as a group do? First, we need to identify the challenge: Are these sincere scientists seeking knowledge and collegiality, and seeking as well to contribute to the store of scientific knowledge out of their own expertise, or are they women seeking only to disrupt male prerogatives? Second, we are pushed by that consideration to define more clearly our own identity: Are we scientists who only happen to be male, or are we men who enjoy one another's company and only happen to dabble in science? Third, we need a normative expression of our identity, which will help us determine it for the present, whether we find this in charter, constitution, or anecdotes. Fourth, the process of interpretation needs some coordination: Who will give voice to the group's self-understanding: the president, secretary, best researcher, oldest member? Fifth, we must consider whose voices will be heard: Are the women to be interviewed, or do we listen only to one another? Sixth, how will this whole process be ordered: Do we meet as a committee of the whole, do we delegate it to a special subgroup, or do we hand it over to the president to decide, since we can't be bothered? Seventh, by what means will the decision be expressed: by vote, by executive decree, by inertia? These questions roughly describe the important elements of group decision making. Not all of them are always present nor always present in equal proportion.

Some groups are shaped by more ultimate values and claim to serve more transcendent purposes than those characterizing science clubs. The reinterpretation of their identity when challenged by change will be more intricate and far-reaching. For a club to admit women as fellow scientists is one thing (not altogether insignificant); but for a "Holy Remnant of the Lord" to admit "Sinners" to communion is quite another. Or, to make the obvious connection, for a male hierarchy to ordain women is similarly shocking. These sorts of decisions will be provoked only by the strongest stimulus and will require the most vigorous sort of interpretative process. For groups whose *task* is understood wholly in terms of *being* a certain way in the world, decisions concerning membership, discipline, and expulsion are inevitably critical, and potentially dangerous to the stability of the group.

In a happy and logical world, one would expect some coherence to the process of decision making, and that the interpretation called forth by challenge would clearly reveal the self-understanding of a group. Explicit decisions ought to reveal the system of values by which a group lives and the framework within which implicit decisions have been made all along.

If a large business corporation, for example, finds itself required to decide whether to continue or stop production of a product, we would expect that something of the business ethos would be revealed by the process of reaching that decision. The "symbolic world" of business understands above all that businesses exist to make profits. The challenge may be posed by a competitor's product cutting into the market. Perhaps this product's declining sales are affecting the market health of an entire line. In either case, the challenge will be interpreted consistently within the group's self-understanding as a profit-making enterprise. A secondary consideration, of course, may be the corporation's "image," how it is perceived by others, especially consumers and investors. It is important to be known as a bold yet trustworthy institution whose stability can be relied on. The juggling of products, therefore, and above all the impression of panic, must be avoided. This consideration as well is directly tied to the profit motive.

The dynamics of decision making in large corporations are doubtless complex, but some factors will carry more weight than others. Whose voice will be heard? Cost-analysis figures and market projections will be studied like runes, but the testimony of assembly-line workers about the pleasure of packaging the product will not be heard. Those who sell the product may not have a voice, but the opinion of those who will buy the product is eagerly sought. The decision will finally be made by a small group of executives who may not even be known by the other members of the group, and whose function has nothing to do with the edification or education of those other members, but only with the proper proportions of money flowing in and out.

Factors not considered in decision making are, in their way, as significant as those which are. No corporation would attribute the decline in a product's popularity to the work of the devil. Nor would a corporation (except in some unfortunate cases) try to discern "God's will" in its struggle to decide whether or not to continue production. These symbols and values are simply not part of the worldview of the corporation, even implicitly. No challenge, therefore, can make them explicit. As for concern with the corporation's "image," it may be packaged in terms of folksy values, but seldom is there the attempt to genuinely maintain continuity with the expressed goals and values of the company's founders. Finally, there is no consideration given to whether or not the product is good for the buyer, in either the immediate or ultimate sense. This group does not exist to define or maintain legitimate human needs; rather, the profit motive drives the group to create needs where none existed.

I do not mean to suggest that there is something bad about this decision-making process in a large corporation. On the contrary, I find it refreshingly straightforward. The implicit values by which the corporation lives are given explicit expression in the making of a concrete decision. One may not like this symbolic world, but it is coherent. It is more disturbing to find groups claiming to live by values different from these, only to learn that they make decisions in a similar way.

My observations on the way groups go about reaching decision are too casual to be sociologically precise. But perhaps they are sufficiently accurate to be provocative and provide a framework for the rest of this discussion. Awareness of the factors at work in the decision-making process of all groups can make our appreciation of the church's practice keener and more realistic. If it is true that decision making is a process wherein a group's identity is revealed; if the challenge to change demands an interpretation in which the implicit self-understanding of the group is made explicit; if this interpretation requires a fresh reading of the group's normative charter; if the voices which are allowed to speak and the voice which speaks most decisively show the structure of the group; then, what do we learn about the nature of the church as we see it reaching decision? Is its proclaimed nature revealed? Is its essential self-understanding given articulation? Or is there a disparity between what the church claims to be and what its way of deciding the future shows it to be?

The answer to these questions will not be found in this book. They can be answered, in fact, only in each of those places where the church is to be found making decisions. I am writing an essay for idealists, after all, and must be more concerned with the "ought" than with the "is." Before I am able to proceed with even that implausible task, however, I must consider some other fundamental notions running throughout the book. What do I mean by church, for example, and where do I think it is found? What is the symbolic world of the church, implicit in all its choices but made explicit by challenge? What is the measure of the church's self-understanding? How is this understanding mediated within the group? These are questions large and unwieldy enough to fill volumes of systematic theology. In the remarks which follow, therefore, you will find not a cautious, even-handed discussion, but a series of idiosyncratic opinions. The opinions, moreover, have been shaped to a considerable degree by the reading of the New Testament to which I will shortly invite you. This exercise contains an inevitable, but I hope not vicious, circularity.

THE CHURCH AS COMMUNITY OF FAITH

It is as hard to find a workable notion of the church as social group as it is to figure out the boundaries of a multinational conglomerate. "Church" is a term applied to many kinds of groups, ranging from the smallest gathering of two or three—"in my name"—at the local level, through a wide variety of sects and denominations, spiraling into ever more complex associations and alliances, all the way to some cosmic understanding of church as "catholic" or "ecumenical," or even to the broadest possible sense, "all those who call on the name of the Lord." The question, Where is the church? not only raises theological hackles but also defies sociological determination.

The competing claims and counterclaims of sects and denominations must be weighed, of course, but we must also look hard to distinguish in each case formal legal structure from a living social group. All groups have structure. As soon as two or three meet more than once and spend any time together, they will, no matter how "equal," begin to develop a sense of order and leadership. Even the most charismatic assembly involves something of "institution." That said, it is not only possible but necessary to distinguish between relative degrees of "life" and "order" in the vast continuum which runs from storefront church to the World Council of Churches. And the more organizational complexity we meet, the more we sense the power of "order" over that of "life." The question, Where is the church? cannot be answered in terms either of organizational charts or ecumenical conferences. It must be answered by another question: Where does the church really live? The church in the strict sense is found where there is a specific group of people who assemble together to call on the name of the Lord in prayer and fellowship.

However much our reflexes have been conditioned to do so, it is a mistake to think of the church first of all in terms of a worldwide organization or alliance of organizations. The decision-making process there, at the ecumenical or world council level, is far removed from the living pulse of God's people. International and interdenominational conversation is important, and must be considered. It should be considered, however, in the last place, not in the first.

The church in its first and living sense means the local assembly, God's convocation in a particular time and place. The doctrine of the church must begin at this local level. So, therefore, should the study of how the church makes decisions. Why? Because it is only at the local level that we can legitimately speak of a "community" at all. Where there is no possibility for face-to-face interaction among the members of a group, then it has ceased to be a community. It has begun to change from organism to organization. The promise of Jesus was to be where two or three were gathered in his name (Matt. 18:20). Certainly, there can be more than two or three. But the promise implies that there is a physical "gathering." Beyond a certain number, such "gathering" becomes difficult. If the church does not live first at this local level, it does not live at all.

Looked at in this way, the church can be recognized as an intentional community. People belong to the church because they choose to belong. The church may practice infant baptism, or even speak of being "born into" the faith. But the community exists in active form because of the present conscious commitment of its members. All churches distinguish between "membership rolls" and "active members," and the distinction is appropriate. It points to the dividing line between legal entity and living organism.

The church's own symbolic understanding, we know, qualifies this identification as an intentional community by claiming that it is called into existence by God. Even as a response to God, however, the choice of individual members makes the church exist at any given moment.

Like other communities constituted by choice, the church has a set of symbols its members share with varying degrees of awareness and commitment. This symbolic world is sometimes simply called "faith," and those who belong to the community are called "believers" or "the faithful." A shorthand for the complex system of creeds and convictions which expresses the church's symbolic world is "the faith." Thus the church can fairly be called a community of faith.

There are different views even within the church concerning the exclusiveness of this communal set of symbols. Some say that this thing called "faith" is found only within the boundaries of the visible community. Others claim that it is found wherever people seek God, even if they cannot share the worship and fellowship of other believers. Still others (and I) hold that genuine faith is found at least implicitly outside the visible church. Indeed, a fundamental function of the church as social group is to make explicit in the world what is implied by the stirrings of hearts everywhere for ultimate truth, and therefore for the true God.

Just as faith can be found outside this group, so also within the group faith is found in the most diverse forms and degrees of health. "Faith" does not describe the finished response of all in the group so much as the norm for those responses, which always fall short of the one for whom they reach.

If we identify the church as a community of faith, the process of decision making ought to make the structures and implications of this response to reality called "faith" more explicit. *Reaching decision in the church should be an articulation of faith.* To see how this might be so, we need to look more closely at this term which is central to the church's identity.

[handwritten margin note: As should decisions in life be.]

FAITH AS THE OBEDIENT HEARING OF GOD

Just as it is important to locate and identify the church as a living organism, so is it helpful to begin with the primary meaning of "faith" from which other meanings derive. Like the term "church," it can have several meanings or senses. It can refer to the whole symbolic universe of the Christian tradition. More narrowly, it can mean the "structure of belief" succinctly summarized in creeds and confessions. "Faith" is also used to describe personal commitment. This use has two distinct emphases. One way of understanding the commitment is in terms of intellectual conviction. Faith is seen as the assent of the mind (and heart) to revealed truths. This is a legitimate and important understanding of faith, but it is still secondary and derivative.

Faith in its proper and active sense describes the response of one person to another in trust and obedience. It is a deeply responsive hearing of another's word, or call. Theological faith is the response by a human being to the call of God, that is, to the Word of God as it is revealed in the fabric of worldly existence. The opposite of such theological faith is idolatry. Idolatry is a way of responding to existence which says that the world we see is all there is. Idolatry flees the terror of contingency and attempts to seize hold of life as a possession. Faith is the response to existence which says that the one who is not seen is most real, and that although contingent, we are established in being every moment by the power of God.

At every moment, God calls us beyond our partial life and perceptions to the experience and knowledge of Godself. Faith is that directing of human freedom which says "yes" both to God and to the human condition. In so doing, it recognizes that part of the human condition, never fully overcome, is the desire to rest in what we can claim as our own. It recognizes as well that the call of God is to a freedom which is frightening in its capacity to possess us but not to be possessed by us.

In the response called faith, the human person asserts that God is not only "real," but that God is what is most real. God is not a vague idea, left over when everything is counted, but is active and alive, and intrudes into human existence—into my existence—not only in the past but also in the present; not only gently but sometimes with rude force; not only in experienced presence but also in experienced absence; not alone in good but also in evil. God creates the world and all that is in it, from nothing, every minute, so that the world and all its peoples might, above the abyss, trust the hand which holds and obey the voice which calls us, and sing, "You are our maker, and to you belongs the glory!"

Because God intrudes into the comfortable space we cling to for self-definition and calls us out to a wider truth, divine revelation continues in our world. God acts now. And since God's activity is meaningful, the Word of God is continually spoken and requires hearing. Faith says that God did not stop speaking when the prophets died, nor even when God's Word was enfleshed in Jesus Christ. Faith asserts that God's Word is enunciated in every age and in every human life by the work of God's Holy Spirit.

At the same time, faith cannot pretend that God's Word is clear and easily available to human understanding. Because it is the Word of the one who moves beyond human grasp and avoids human naming, and because it is a Word spoken in and through the circumstances of worldly life, it is ambiguous and requires cautious and humble deciphering. The first interpretation takes place in the response of faith itself. The obedience of faith demands the scrutiny of God's Word here and now. What in this context is the legitimate human project, and what the project of God which calls all others into account? In few cases is such scrutiny easy; in some it seems nearly impossible. In the powerful disturbance of our complacency, we may recognize the Holy, but that does not yet yield knowledge of the call it makes to us.

Since God calls us anew every moment, the response of faith is never-ending. This hearing demands an asceticism of attentiveness. There is never a moment before death when faith can say, "Enough, it is finished," for the Word of God to each individual is not fully spoken until that death. God's Word unfolds with every breath we breathe. Faith moves constantly from death to life: death to our prior understanding, footholds, and securities; and life, given freely each moment by another. A perilous progress. For this reason, we can recognize Jesus as the pioneer and perfecter of our faith. He moved in obedience to the death of the cross, and when he wished to live on his own terms, he said "yes" to the one who called him.

Where the church exists as something more than institution or ethical society, it is marked by this kind of faith. The church is a paschal community, dying in order to live. In the lives of its individual members, faith seeks to discern the call of God in their particular circumstances. As a group, the community as well seeks to discern the Word spoken to this people in the challenges of the present moment. The identity of the church is always being shaped by its response to God's call in the context of its worldly life.

The relevance of this for the present discussion should be clear: The implicit choices of the group, which the challenge to change ought to make explicit, are the choices of faith for God's Word. This means, in turn, that the process of making decisions in the church will evoke and involve the interpretation of God's Word. The church is called into existence in the first place, sustained, and addressed by the activity of God both within it and outside it. The church believes, therefore, that—however darkly—it is being called as a group by the working of God in its members. This working of God requires scrutiny, discernment. Is this truly God's Word which is being spoken to us in these circumstances, or a counterfeit of that Word? Discernment, the process of sorting, evaluating, and distinguishing among competing voices, is already a kind of decision.

There is another sense in which God's Word requires discernment by the church. We cannot recognize the action of God in the present as God's action unless we have some knowledge of God's work in the past. The Word of God in Scripture, therefore, is an essential aspect of the church's discernment in decision making. It is in that Word—that set of symbols and stories—that the church finds the grammar for deciphering the Word spoken here and now. The observation leads us to the role of theology in the life of the church, which is the life of faith.

THEOLOGY AS THE ARTICULATION OF FAITH IN THE CHURCH

Faith is first of all not attachment to a body of doctrines but a process of responding in obedience and trust to God's Word. God has given us the possibility of hearing the Word, since it was spoken in the humanity of Jesus, which we share, and since it continues to be spoken through the Holy Spirit, which dwells in us. So also theology is first of all not the study of doctrines, but a process of reflection on this response of faith. The classic definition of theology, "faith seeking understanding" (*fides quaerens intellectus*), remains always valid. Faith seeks to understand the one to whom it responds. It also, thereby, seeks to understand itself, and the implications of being so called and so gifted to respond.

Theology is an articulation of faith in at least three ways. First, theology articulates faith in the sense of "giving voice" to faith. Part of theology's task is tending the story of faith and keeping alive the possibility of its continuation. Second, theology articulates faith by showing its structure: How do the various aspects of this living response fit together? Third, theology articulates faith by searching out the connections between this most fundamental and pervasive response to reality, and all the other responses life demands. If we say "yes" to God, what does this imply for saying "yes" to the human condition and "yes" to the world?

The faith that seeks understanding is not just the faith of each individual alone; it is the faith of the church. This statement can be understood in two ways. Conventionally, the "faith of the church" designates precisely the creeds, doctrines, and traditions which the theologian would study. But if we understand the faith of the church in dynamic terms, then the search of theology for understanding involves the active discernment of the responses to God being made by individuals as they together, as church, seek to decide in favor of God.

Who is qualified for this? It cannot be the task only of appointed or even of gifted individuals within the assembly. The theological task is implied by the very life of faith itself. Every Christian is therefore called to do theology in this sense. Every Christian must seek an understanding of his or her response to God and the implications of that response for the rest of life. Everyone in the church must exercise discernment concerning the response of the church as a whole to the challenge of God's Word.

The church itself is the locus of theology. It is not so just as the place where a theologian happens to work. Theology is, rather, a task to be taken up by the church as such. Because everyone in the church is required to interpret his or her life before God, everyone in this community is also required to do theology. Everything else we mean by theology derives from this fundamental sense. Otherwise, the "faith" which seeks understanding is removed from the pulse of human life, and therefore from God's revelation in the world.

That everyone in the church is called to do theology in this way does not mean that some people in the community do not exercise this ministry in a special way. A look at other articulations of the church's life helps us realize how ministries make explicit for the group what is implicit in the lives of all. In worship, the leader gives voice and gesture to the adoration in the hearts of all. If only the leader prays, there is no community worship, but only private piety performed in public. Likewise in works of mercy, those who reach out to the needy in the church's name make explicit the openhandedness implicit in the lives of its members; otherwise, the symbolization of the community's faith is counterfeit. So with theology: All Christians are required to interpret their lives before God, but some in the church have the ability to make these diverse interpretations available to all, and to articulate more formally the implications of the choices being made by all the members.

Above all, the theologian helps the church to form and understand its response as a group, helps it pull together the many individual interpretations of God's Word into a communal discernment which prepares for decision. The theologian may be preacher or teacher, may be ordained or not, may be now one person, now another. But the theologian's interpretation of how God is calling us as a group will be alive and pertinent only if the same process of interpretation is going on in the lives of individual believers within the community. The case is the same as that with worship and work: Without the implicit process, the explicit gesture is meaningless. But here, the situation is even more acute.

If the people are not themselves seeking to determine the Word of God in the tangle of their individual and shared lives, how can they discern the accuracy and adequacy of the theologian's interpretation of that Word for the group? The church as a group, as a gathering of believers, must test the Spirit's movement. This means to test the word of interpretation spoken in the assembly concerning the movement of the Spirit. If only one is interpreting, then the process fails. In such an atmosphere, both false prophecy and demagoguery flourish. This also means that a theologian who is not in contact with the faith-life of an actual church runs the danger of having nothing to say, and of becoming a theologian in name only. The discernment of the "practical life" of the Christian community is the cutting edge of theology. The more intellectually elaborate studies of doctrinal and systematic theology depend on a healthy pastoral theology for their life.

When theology is understood in this fashion as a process of interpreting God's Word within the believing community, the unending nature of its task becomes clear. Theology needs to be renewed in every age, for the call of faith is always new. The subject matter of theology is not only the record of how God acted in the past, but above all how God is acting in the present. Furthermore, the call of God comes to us in the structures of worldly life, which themselves are constantly in flux. The implications of the faith response, therefore, cannot be fixed absolutely, but require an ever-renewed discernment by the community of faith. We change, and the structures of our world change; but more than that, the God who calls us is alive and moves ahead of us at every moment. Theology is always a catch-up ball game. As the obedience of faith demands a constant alertness to the movement of God's Spirit in the life of an individual, so does theology call for constant attentiveness to the work of the Spirit in the church's life here and now.

The theologian, then, is one within the church who articulates for all what has first been experienced by everyone who believes. By such articulation, the theologian reminds the community of its own deepest convictions, which are always in danger of being lost in the welter of worldly life. The theologian can remind the church of them only if they are alive for the theologian as well. The theologian is one who interprets his or her own life in the following terms.

First, God is alive and active in the world. Second, God here and now intrudes into human existence in powerful, sometimes frightening, and frequently ambiguous ways. Third, this intrusion presents the call of God to obedience and trust. Fourth, as the call is never-ending, so is the obedience of faith never finished, so that the church can never say, "enough." Fifth, the possibility of our identifying the work of God in the circumstances of the moment depends on our knowledge and understanding of God's activity in the past. Sixth, the possibility for this recognition is given by the symbols and stories of the Bible. This last point suggests another way of describing the function of theology within the life of faith.

THEOLOGY AND THE NARRATIVE OF EXPERIENCE

One of the ways the theologian serves the church is by helping it to tell its story. If we only appreciate storytelling as a pleasant diversion, we will not grasp the importance of this function. The study of societies—simple and complex alike—shows us that although some forms of storytelling do serve a recreational purpose, others perform a more fundamental, *re-creational* role within the life of communities, shaping both the group and its understanding of reality. This kind of storytelling has to do with personal and group identity. The story of my life—if I can tell it—reveals who I am. Our communal story—if we can give it shape—tells others, and first of all ourselves, how we have come to be who we are.

In the life of groups we find such storytelling in the myths of origin and those which accompany rites of passage. In the life of individuals, such personal storytelling is found in confession or therapy, where the telling of the story whole not only expresses a stage of intimacy and trust but also reveals at once to the other and to the self who one is.

Such personal and revelatory storytelling is an ordered form of personal or group memory, and memory *is* identity. Amnesia is a terrible affliction precisely because the loss of the past means the loss of the present as well. If I cannot remember who I have been, then I do not know who I now am. The same is true for groups: Forgetting our past means ignorance of our present and the forfeiture of our future.

It is here we find the critical function of tradition for the life of groups. The real business of tradition is not the securing of the past, but the ensuring of a future. Only when we know how the story has run to this point can we responsibly decide how the plot might now unfold. Humans are creatures who make up their stories as they go along. In them, they find both their identity and meaning. But it is not a random process. The story can only move forward as story, that is, with meaning, when it appropriates the past. Otherwise, there is not really change. Where there is no continuity, there is only meaningless movement.

Personal storytelling inevitably involves selection and shaping. Because we **are** telling the story of our experience—trying to order our memory of ourselves as we have existed in the world—and because our experience continues, we are constantly revising our story. Our past looks different to us at every moment. Our present experience influences our selection of past events we remember as significant. Because I am having a miserable day, I remember that "my mother told me I'd have days like this." The pressure of the present makes various points of the past pertinent. The same force causes us to shape that memory of the past into forms usable in the present. My mother probably never said in so many words, "You'll have days like that," but from all her care and counsel in the past, I shape my memory of her into this more universal and pithy shape. We make up our stories as we go along, and it is always a revisionist history. As with individuals, so with groups.

Experience and interpretation affect each other in this kind of storytelling. My story as I know it up to now—the way I understand myself in the world—gives me the categories for perceiving my present experience. No matter how powerful or profound, no experience is utterly naked. Already in the very act of sensation, we are interpreting on the basis of our past perceptions. We "see" the grass growing, and not the earth receding, because that is the way our story runs. We extend our hand to another for shaking, rather than reach for a weapon or flee, because our story causes us to see the outstretched hand of the other as a friendly gesture. When the handshake is friendly, my perceptions get reinforced, and my story requires no rereading.

But the effect of experience on interpretation can take another form. Experiences can be so radical or powerful or surprising that they not only stretch, but snap our categories of perception. If the other person grabs my hand and claps it into a handcuff, or if he cuts my hand, I must reconsider the place of handshakes in my story. So every challenge to change forces us to reread our story with new eyes.

Of all the stories humans can tell, the most fundamental one is surely their religious history, the story of their experience of God in the world. Strangely, however, this story is seldom told by individuals in the faith assembly. And when it is, it is unfortunately done in a manner which shows little reflective understanding. Yet, if God is alive and active at every moment, and if people are being called to faith by God's activity, then there must be such a story, at least implicitly, in the lives of all those who believe. Why is it not being told? And why do those who overcome embarrassment and try to speak this story find that they do not even have the words to tell it? We will look more closely at these questions in the last chapters of this book.

For now, I simply state my conviction that one of the tasks of theology is to help the church both hear and then tell its story. The theologian therefore needs to interpret both parts of the story: that which has already been told and that which is being spoken. The theologian seeks to make explicit the shape of God's Word being spoken to the church in the present circumstances, and how the church's decisions might continue the story of God's people. To do this, the theologian must listen to the narratives of those who believe—including the theologian's own story. The theologian also needs to interpret the story which has gone before: How has God worked among the people in the past? By what means can we recognize, if not God's face, then the trail of God's mercy and justice as they grace and frighten us? Without the means of perception given us by the story of our past history with God, we shall not be able to discern God's Word being spoken now. Without knowing of the

Holy Spirit, its fruits, and its transforming power, how can we perceive the Spirit creating and sanctifying among us now?

We should make no mistake: The experience of God or the experience of God's absence is not accessible for casual perusal. It requires careful attention and delicate diagnosis. The process of discernment is risk-filled and never self-validating. The interpretation of the present moment is perilous, prone to error, always in need of renewal and revision. But such interpretation is the absolutely fundamental and necessary task of theology in the church. Without it, there is no subject matter.

THE NORMATIVE FRAMEWORK OF THE SCRIPTURE

The first part of the story is equally difficult to interpret. Not only is our shared Christian story a long one, but it is varied, fragmented, and filled with conflict and contradiction. Parts of it are lost in darkness, parts of it distorted by sin and neglect. There is everywhere shadow. The theologian therefore looks to some part of the story that can stand as normative for the rest, that is, which can give a frame for the proper understanding of the story which precedes us, and for the story which unfolds as we tell it. The theologian and other believers claim to find this normative framework in the canon of the Scripture, the compositions of the Old and New Testaments.

The theologian seeks there the interpretative tools for discerning the story of the present. The decision to regard the canon of the Old and New Testaments as normative—as providing a sort of measure for authentic life before God—does not result from scientific inquiry, or from historical research. The decision to regard these historically conditioned documents as having a normative force for every age of the church is a decision of faith. It is preeminently a church decision. In fact, it is one of the decisions that constitute the church as such in every generation. The canon and the church are correlative in this sense: Without the community regarding them as addressing it in an authoritative and normative way, these ancient writings would not be Scripture. On the other hand, without such a fixed frame of understanding, which mediates the identity of the community from age to age, there would not exist any historical community identifiable as the church in the first place. It is an expression of the church's faith to regard these writings as prophetic for every age, and therefore as speaking God's Word. Canonization, therefore, is more than the residue of past decisions. It is a decision renewed by the church every time it reads these writings in the assembly for worship; when it looks to these writings alone as its unmeasured measure of self-understanding; when it allows these writings to question and interpret its present existence in a way it will let no other writings do.

As one who articulates the faith of the church, the theologian asserts this authoritative function of the Scripture in the life of the community, and in the reaching of decisions. It is not the theologian's role to decide *how* texts are to be normative. The theologian serves the church by allowing the text from the past and the text of the present to enter mutual interpretation. The theologian thereby helps provide the context for the discernment of God's Word now by allowing that Word to be shaped and questioned by God's Word in the Scripture. When that Word is brought into conversation with the present, it also becomes reread and reinterpreted because of God's continuing revelation in the stories of the people. The theologian does not interpret the Scripture alone, any more than the theologian interprets the moment alone. The church discerns and decides on behalf of God. The theologian helps this happen by allowing the Scripture to speak to life, and the word of life to speak to the Scripture, and this within the assembly of God's people.

These comments presuppose the availability of the writings in the Old and New Testaments for theological reflection within the assembly. To say that the Old and New Testaments provide the symbols and stories necessary for the discernment of God's Word in the stories of people today, implies both the pertinence of these writings to life and the perception of that pertinence by the people. Neither the presupposition nor implication may be valid for many churches or even for many theologians today. It is to that problem we now turn: How can the Scripture be made available for the church seeking to reach decision, and thereby express its identity as a community of faith?

I will not even try to answer the question in general, for I do not think there is a general answer. Rather the question can only be answered for particular writings in particular situations. Attempts at making the Scripture relevant for contemporary readers—the art of hermeneutics—have usually dealt with the private reading of the texts by individuals. But the Scripture is first of all a church collection. These texts were written to be read before many hearers at worship, and so they are read in the church today. They are also read for purposes of public discussion and discernment. The Scripture as Scripture is appropriated by a community. Therefore, the act of interpretation (the hermeneutical process) must also involve the community. Another tendency of hermeneutics has been to search for one way of making the texts relevant. It has sought a mode of mediating the texts of Scripture by one rational construct or another. As a result, those texts which do not fit the construct do not get read, and are called "irrelevant." But there can be no one way of mediating texts so diverse to an audience so diverse as the church. The writings were written at different times and places for differing purposes. And they speak through different literary forms. Theological interpretation in the church, therefore, must take seriously the diversity of the writings in the canon, and the diversity of the church not only in every age, but even in every locale in the same age. The relevance of texts will be proved, not by philosophical or rhetorical analysis, but by the use of them in the churches. The first theological task is to allow the conversation to start. How the parts of the story will connect depends on the discernment and decision of particular communities in specific places.

In the next two chapters, two debated questions concerning the role of the New Testament (specifically) within the life and theology of the church will be addressed. The first has to do with the authority of the text, the second with the irreducible diversity of voices found within the canon. Rather than regard diversity as a problem for biblical authority or theology, I find it a great gift from God to the church.

CHAPTER 2

DEBATES: THE AUTHORITY OF THE NEW TESTAMENT IN THE CHURCH

The question of whether and how the Bible has authority for the life of the church is one that needs to be faced squarely and candidly. No issue has more potential for subverting otherwise useful theological conversations. No issue tends to polarize Christians more decisively. The range of available options, furthermore, is extensive. At one extreme are those whose position is avowedly conservative: They insist that the authority of the Bible is absolute and unequivocal; indeed, they locate that authority in the Bible's every statement. At the other extreme are those who consider the Bible as a text whose authority must be rejected if the true liberation of oppressed peoples is to be accomplished; only those statements that agree with the reader's ideological position are allowed to be heard. In between these extremes are many other and more nuanced options.

When placed in this context, my position on biblical authority undoubtedly has a "liberal" character, even though on most issues touching interpretation I am conservative. On the issue of canon and church in particular—as will become clear shortly—I am profoundly traditional. Concerning the *use* of the Bible in the church, nevertheless, my position can fairly be described as liberal, because it presumes and encourages that liberty of the children of God given by the Spirit: "Where the Spirit of the Lord is, there is freedom" (2 Cor. 3:17). Freedom is not, however, to be equated with slovenliness or carelessness. Indeed, faith's freedom is the most rigorous of all asceticisms.

My position is liberal as well because it emphasizes the dialectical relationship between text and readers. But what texts? Some limitations of the subject are imperative. I address myself here primarily to the authority of the New Testament. I will touch only tangentially on the authority of Torah, asserting that in the context of the church, all readings of Torah must pass at least implicitly through the prism of the New Testament.

I am considering only the question of the New Testament's authority as read text. I leave aside all the fascinating but distracting ways authority is ascribed to the book as sacred object. The Bible is treated as authority of some sort when we incense it, carry it in procession, open it with closed eyes and point to a passage, wave it in preaching, bow before it, cover it with jewels, swear by it in court. In the Christian religion, the Bible has undoubtedly had more authority in this talismanic way than as read text. Bell, book, and candle have seldom paused for solemn exegesis. But I bracket this too-little explored aspect of religious phenomenology in order to address the authority of the text as read.

The meaning of the word "authority" is also problematic, but takes on some specificity by being restricted to the text as read. The New Testament supplies a number of possible antecedents, ranging from *dynamis* with its nuance of impersonal power, to *exousia*, with its suggestion of freedom. At the very least, if we are speaking of the authority of a text as text, then we cannot mean something that simply inheres in the book as book; we must mean a quality that is ascribed to the act of reading the text.

The most important preliminary consideration is the framework within which the New Testament is read. The understanding of authority I advance here makes sense only within a very specific context of reading. To establish that context as rapidly as possible, I will repeat a series of points I made at the end of my book *Writings of the New Testament: An Interpretation* (Philadelphia: Fortress Press, 1986), which I call "canonical theses."

SOME CANONICAL THESES

1. The canon of Scripture is the church's working bibliography. Whatever else is read and studied by individual Christians in private, these writings are used by the assembly as such for debating and defining its identity. These are, therefore, the public documents of the church. They are public in the sense that their first use is to be read aloud in worship. They are also public because they offer themselves to the entire community's debate and discernment.

2. The canon is more than the residuum of a historical process. It is a faith decision for the church to make in every age and place. The

acceptance of these specific writings by a community—not by council but in liturgical use—is the most fundamental identity decision the church makes. The choice excludes contemporary writings that would make a similar claim for allegiance, and thereby asserts continuity with the community's past, and assumes responsibility for transmitting the same measure to the church in the future.

3. The canon and the church are, therefore, correlative concepts. The canon establishes discrete writings from the past as this community's Scripture. Without a church there can be no canon; without canon there is no Scripture in the fullest sense. As the church stands under the norm of Scripture in every age, finding life and meaning in the reading of it, so do these writings find their realization as Scripture by being so read by a community, age after age, as the measure of its life and meaning.

4. It is the nature of a canon to be closed. An unlimited canon is no measure, any more than a foot ruler can gain inches and still be a foot ruler. Because it is closed, the canon can perform the function of mediating a specific identity through successive ages of the church. Because the church today reads the same writings as were read by Polycarp and Augustine and Aquinas and Luther and Barth, it remains identifiably the same community, and on that basis can debate with those earlier readers their interpretations and realizations of that identity. Only a steady measure can provide such continuity. The discovery of a lost apostolic letter would occasion excitement but could not be included in the canon, for it had never shaped the identity of the catholic church.

5. Because the canon is closed and exclusive, it can be catholic, that is, have universal and enduring pertinence. This is only an apparent paradox. A measure that can be altered by addition or subtraction at any time or place has no capacity to address every time and place.

6. What distinguishes the Scripture scholar and theologian from the historian of ideas or student of literature is the effective recognition of the canon. For history and literature as such, the concept of canon is meaningless, except as a convenient categorization, or as the recognition that a certain group of writings achieved classical status at a certain time. These affirmations, however, fall short of asserting the distinctive interrelationship between specific texts and a living community over an extended period of time that is essential to the notion of canon.

7. The ecclesial decision to regard these writings as Scripture bears with it the recognition that they have a peculiar and powerful claim on the lives of individuals and above all on the community as a whole. The church asserts that it does not control these writings but that they in a very real sense control it, by providing the definitive frame for its

Need for an unchanging canon

36

self-understanding. Within the church, the critical questions posed to the texts by a reader are far less significant than the critical questions the texts pose to the reader.

8. Implicit in the recognition of the canonical writings as Scripture is the acknowledgment that they not only speak in the voice of their human authors but also speak for an Other. The New Testament speaks prophetically to every age. Analytic to the concept of prophecy is the speaking of God's Word. These texts play a critical role in the process of God's revelation. Within their time-conditioned words and symbols, which come from many persons in the past, there speaks as well the singular Word of God, which endures through the ages. This conviction can be expressed by the statement that the texts are "divinely inspired," for to speak of the Word of God is to speak as well by implication of the work of God's Spirit.

9. Divine inspiration is one of the ways of expressing the unique authority Christians attribute to these writings. Explanations and interpretations of inspiration obviously vary widely, ranging from psychological theories that virtually equate it with literary inspiration, through metaphysical distinctions between primary and secondary causes, to attributing the whole creative process of composition within the social context of earliest Christianity to the real but subtle working of the Holy Spirit as part of the constitutive act of creating church.

10. Since the canon consists of a disparate collection of writings, with both the Old Testament and New Testament forming the Christian Bible, it resists reduction to any single unifying principle imposed from without as much as it lacks any explicit unifying principle within. If it excludes by its nature any "canon within the canon," it certainly also resists any conceptual mold that either relativizes or removes the texts themselves in all their hard particularity. The resistance applies as well to any "biblical theology." In all its forms, biblical theology is simply another attempt to reduce the many to one by means of some abstract unifying principle, whether it is denominated salvation history or justification or liberation or kerygma or *regula fidei* or narrativity or existential decision. All such principles demand the selection of some texts as *a priori* more central and governing than others. All fit the writings themselves to frames of greater or lesser abstraction. The canon resists such attempts precisely because it is made up of multiple and irreducible writings which cannot without distortion be shaped into a static symbolic system.

On the other hand, the canon opens itself to the doing of theology in the church, which is another sort of enterprise altogether. In theology properly so called, the experience of God in human lives and events is articulated and brought into a faithful dialogue with all the writings of the Old and New Testaments, not in an attempt to fix their meaning but in a living conversation that ranges freely and leads to surprising results.

11. Since the canon consists of the public documents of a community which have as their natural context proclamation in the liturgical assembly, the church requires a hermeneutic appropriate to the nature of the canon. Such a hermeneutic would not be concerned primarily with the reading of the text by individuals for their pleasure or transformation. This sort of reading has had all sorts of interpretative models from allegory through existential interpretation to reader-response. None of these need be rejected. Freedom and fantasy open the minds and hearts of people. But such models of interpretation scarcely reach the neighbor, and do not provide a way of reading the texts in their primary function, which is to mediate the identity of the church as church.

These canonical theses argue that what is needed in the church is a properly *ecclesial hermeneutic*, one that places the writings in their proper canonical context and that involves the entire faith community in the interpretative process. For such a hermeneutic to work, there must be the active discernment of the work of God in the lives of believers today, raised to the level of a narrative of faith; there must be, at the same time, the active discernment of the canonical texts in the light of these experiences and narratives. This process of discernment must occur in a public context that enables discussion, debate, disagreement, and decision. In this creative if tension-filled context, the canonical witnesses can again shape the identity of the Christian community.

A MIDRASHIC MODEL FOR AN ECCLESIAL HERMENEUTIC

The formation of an ecclesial hermeneutic should follow the process by which the writings of the New Testament themselves came into existence, and allow the dialectic of experience and interpretation to come alive again. The New Testament writings came into being in the first place by means of a process best termed *midrashic*. The term *midrash* is used within the rabbinic tradition to describe the entire complex process of searching (Heb. *darash*) Torah in the light of contemporary circumstance, for insight into either law or life. In early Christianity, the tensions between sacred texts and powerful religious experiences forced new understandings and eventually a restructured symbolic world.

It is the fundamental conviction of faith that such powerful religious experiences continue to occur in our world. People continue to encounter the living God, however dark and oblique the ways in which they do so might be. But as the church today seeks to deal with the tensions between text and experience, it is not only the symbolic world of Torah which requires negotiation but also the texts of the New Testament itself; this symbolic world too must be reshaped and renewed by the continuing experience of the Spirit in and outside the church, and come to new clarity in the interpretative context of the community.

Just as midrash is a category that enables us to understand the process of the text's creation, so is it a category that enables us to move in the direction of a properly ecclesial hermeneutic. The Christian church can again learn something from Judaism and regard the New Testament canon as analogous to the Talmud—the authoritative collection of midrashic activity completed around the fifth or sixth century C.E. As the Talmud was a crystallization of a long history of interpretation of Torah mediated by new experiences, which became authoritative for the Jewish tradition not as the replacement of Torah but as the inescapable prism through which Torah would be read and understood, so can the New Testament writings be regarded as crystallizations of reflection on Torah in the light of the experience of Jesus the crucified Messiah and risen Lord. The New Testament writings remain authoritative and normative for the Christian tradition not as the replacement of Torah, but as the indispensable prism through which Torah is to be read and understood.

There is this important difference: In the Talmud there are not separate writings, but a diversity of voices, whereas in the New Testament there is diversity both of voice and of literary form (see the next chapter for a consideration of this issue). But there is also this even more critical similarity: In the study of Talmud, one never listens to only one voice or authority. One never follows the views of Rabbi Judah through every tractate or of Rabbi Eliezer on every topic. Nor does the study of Talmud yield a single abstractable answer that need not be reinterpreted in the light of changing circumstances. Indeed, the whole point of midrash is to hear the various voices in all their conflicts and disagreements, for it is precisely in those elements of plurality and even disharmony that the texts open themselves to new meaning, so that they are allowed to speak to the disharmonies and disjunctions of contemporary life.

In just such a fashion, Christians should learn to read the canon of the New Testament, not in the search for an essential core or purified canon within the canon, not within the frame of a single abstract principle, but in a living conversation with all the writings in their diversity and divergence.

[handwritten margin note: Then did some canonical authors miss the mark so that they must be put in tension with others?]

39

MEANINGS OF AUTHORITY

Within the context of church and canon, then, at least three critical aspects of the New Testament's authority can be distinguished.

A. The New Testament as Author

Of first importance for the Christian community is the New Testament's ability to *author;* that is, to create a certain identity in its readers, to bring a Christian community into existence or renew it. Whether read in the assembly or by lonely individuals in motel rooms and prison cells, the writings can shape a new and distinctive consciousness, empower capacities that were previously not there. The New Testament has transformative power. There is nothing magical or even specifically theological in this: The reading of Shakespeare, after all, has created poets and lovers of poetry. What *is* specifically theological is the conviction of the church that this authoring power of the Scripture is activated by the Holy Spirit. All texts can transform, but these texts transform according to the mind of Christ (1 Cor. 2:16).

It is in this identity-formative function that the New Testament has the greatest degree of unanimity within the variety of its literary forms and distinctive authorial perspectives. The writings converge on the matter of identity: the meaning of life before God in light of a crucified and raised Messiah whose Spirit enlivens a character expressed by faith, hope, and love. Faith, hope, and love, in turn, are enacted by the messianic pattern of life for others that governs both individual consciousness and the dynamics of interaction in the community. These are not the special insights of Paul or James or John, but ground all the writings at the deep level of implicit agreement that enabled a *regula fidei* (rule of faith, creed) to be constructed in the first place.

Here is where the New Testament is most reliable and trustworthy, most deserving of the designation *inerrant,* for it is in this realm of what Roman Catholicism in another connection calls "faith and morals," that we touch on the real subject matter of the New Testament writings, their "intentionality." Because now this aspect and now that aspect of authentic Christian identity is found in the respective writings, they must all be read for that identity properly to be formed. A Christian consciousness based solely on the Gospel of John would surely be distorted in the direction of exclusivism and sectarianism without the saving irony of the Gospel of Mark. A Christian identity based solely on Paul as purveyor of righteousness by faith alone would be distorted in the direction of pietism without the challenge to practical morality posed by the Letter of James.

This identity function is fulfilled best and most reliably when the documents are read in liturgy, where the ritual of the community and the critical reflection of preaching alike can work as coauthors of identity. The power of these texts to form identity is certainly as powerful—perhaps even more so because undiluted—in the case of private reading, but it is also more dangerous because unconditioned by community debate and discernment. What Paul said of prophecy in the assembly should apply as well to the private reading of Scripture: "Let all discern" (1 Cor. 14:29).

B. The New Testament as Authorizer

The New Testament canon also provides authorization for its own interpretation. The identity function moves toward definition and integrity—this pattern of life is authentically Christian, that one is not—but the authorizing function moves toward freedom, the empowerment of the New Testament readers themselves. By "authority" here I mean what the Latin term *auctoritas* includes as example and warrant. The New Testament provides its readers with examples of ways in which authoritative texts can freely be reread in light of new experience and the working of the Spirit—without thereby ceasing to be normative. The most obvious example is the rereading of Torah in the light of the crucified Messiah. The New Testament writers do not seem to think the authority of Torah makes it immune from interpretation, even of the boldest sort. Paul's "history of salvation" in Romans 9–11 appears nowhere in Torah itself and is legitimated only by his conviction that Messiah is the *telos* of Torah (Rom. 10:4). On the same basis, Paul denies the authority of Torah as commandment while upholding its authority as narrative in Galatians 3–4. The hermeneutical options of midrash, typology, and allegory so important for the history of Christian interpretation are all given by the New Testament itself.

Such freedom of interpretation is applied not only to Torah, but also to the story of Jesus. How else can we account for the development of the Synoptic tradition, in which first the oral tradition is worked into a narrative by Mark, and then reinterpreted in quite divergent ways by Matthew and Luke without the suppression of the earlier version? Or how account for the idiosyncratic reworking of the Gospel tradition by John, accepted side by side in the canon with those other three? As historians we observe the *exousia* exercised by the first Christian writers, but we hesitate—far more than did our ancestors Clement and Origen—to appropriate it ourselves.

The New Testament also provides *exempla* that authorize certain hermeneutical activities in the church, such as the process of reaching decision. Later in this book, I will analyze the narrative account in Acts 10–15 that recounts the decision to grant Gentiles full status in the church, not simply as a historical record, but as a scriptural warrant for the church in our own age reaching decisions in the same fashion: by hearing the narratives of faith based in the experiences of present-day believers, and allowing debate and discernment of those narratives to lead to new understandings of Scripture itself.

C. The New Testament as a Collection of *Auctoritates*

A third meaning of authority applies to the thematic level of the New Testament writings, where the diversity of literary forms and divergence of opinions is most obvious. On any number of issues it is simply impossible to reconcile what New Testament writers have to say on the same subject. The answer to the question, What does the New Testament have to say about X, is often, It depends on what you have read last. If we ask, for example, "What is the Christian attitude toward the State," we must consider at least the chasm between Romans and 1 Peter on one side, and Revelation on the other. If we ask, "What is the proper Christian attitude toward the world," we would have an even more complex range of views, running from the irenicism of 1 Peter, through the intricate "as though not" of Paul, to the radical sectarianism of the Johannine Letters.

We meet the same diversity on other questions, down to and including the best way to describe Jesus, an obvious factor in the internecine battles over christological definitions for some six centuries. If we turn to such practical matters as when and how to baptize, or celebrate the Lord's supper, or organize a community, the sad history of Christianity illustrates just how obviously it is possible to prove anything on the basis of the New Testament, as long as a certain judicious selectivity and suppression of evidence is carried out.

What do we make then of this thematic jumble? In the first place, we exercise common sense and make a healthy distinction. If the New Testament writings agree so powerfully on the shape of Christian identity but differ so much on the specifics of its articulation in the world, this might mean two things: The first is that identity is more important than ritual consistency; the second is that the New Testament actually legitimates a healthy pluralism of practice within the same basic identity.

Within such diversity, in turn, we are allowed to exercise the *exousia* given by the New Testament itself with regard to Torah. We resist the urge to make only one such *auctoritas* (or opinion) normative to the exclusion of others. We avoid the temptation to an easy or false harmonization. Rather, as with the opinions in the Talmud, we enter into a conversation with these diverse views and opinions expressed by the New Testament, finding in their areas of overlap as well as in their points of divergence guidance for our own decisions.

But in the end, none of the options may represent our practice as individuals or as community. What then? If we do not *do* exactly what these statements direct, how can we call them an authority? Because we take them into account. Every Christian community, like every Christian, stands to one degree or another in disagreement with some part of the New Testament. Anyone who claims otherwise is simply lying. The issue of biblical authority, therefore, is not whether it gives a consistent blueprint for every aspect of our lives, or that our lives conform exactly to that blueprint. Given the diversity within the canon, any such claim would be specious. The issue of authority is whether the texts are taken seriously as normative, even when—as is often true—they diverge or even disagree.

Taking the texts seriously means that in our ecclesial—as well as personal—decisions we are willing to take our stand over against as well as under the text. Do we allow divorce in our community despite Jesus' clear condemnation of divorce? Then we do not live in accord with this text. To be faithful to the Scripture, we cannot suppress its reading; we must be able to say *why* we do not live in accord with its clear directive. This means that we must find *authorization* for our position somewhere else in these writings; sometimes we will be given an option by the divergence of another text or by the *exousia* of reinterpretation in the light of new experiences of God's work in human lives and events. The limit to such *exousia*, in turn, is set by the integrity of the individual and community identity as measured by the messianic pattern authored by these same writings.

These observations apply to the other positions we adopt concerning such matters as women pastors, or the equality of women in the household, or to our taking of oaths, or to our equation of Christianity with mental and physical well-being and material comfort and the American way of life. There is no room for sloppiness and shoddiness in these matters. It is not scholarship that demands precision as well as passion in the reading of the New Testament. As John Updike said in another context, "Precision is a function of attention and attention is a function of concern" (*Picked up Pieces*, New York: Knopf, 1975, p. 248). If we are not precise in these things, then we do not care. And carelessness is as good a candidate as any for the sin against the Spirit.

Such, I submit, are the complex ways in which the authority of the New Testament in the church should be understood. My analysis separates levels of normativity, not on the basis of antiquity or authorship, but on the basis of functions. Identity is the presupposition for freedom; the freedom of God's children is more important than conformity. On the other hand, the freedom to read in the way I have suggested is conditioned by a strong view of church and canon. It presupposes that the texts are read as a church when it makes decisions, and that discernment is allowed to take place.

CHAPTER 3

DEBATES: THE LITERARY DIVERSITY OF THE NEW TESTAMENT AND THEOLOGY

The literary diversity of the New Testament is a fact, the dimensions of which become more apparent as sustained literary-critical attention is given to the earliest Christian writings. Not only do the Gospels differ from letters, and letters from apocalyptic, but one Gospel differs from another Gospel in literary structuring, tone, and emphasis; one letter of Paul differs from another in conventional type, mode of argumentation, rhetorical style.

For the critic who reads the New Testament primarily for the evidence it provides of first-century Hellenistic literature, such diversity is only delightful, particularly since the New Testament is so generically unstable, borrowing, reshaping, and shedding forms as it goes. For the historian who reads the New Testament for evidence of early Christian mores or social settings, literary diversity is a difficult but not insurmountable roadblock to be negotiated. Rhetoric must be taken into account before a text can be treated as a source of information.

For those who want to use them in theology, however, the literary diversity of the New Testament writings presents a serious problem. It is so above all for the one who defines theology in terms of an ecclesial, that is, a communal and faith-defined, process for which the *literal* meaning of the text is an essential component, and who thinks of the New Testament writings as discrete literary compositions whose diverse genres and rhetorical conventions demand consideration for any responsible reading. Literary diversity is only apparent to those who can see the writings as a whole; a factor only for those who read them with the expectation of hearing not only their human author's voice, but in some fashion, God's Word. I will argue here that the literary diversity of the New Testament is an open invitation to theology as communal discernment of the will of God. Theology so understood is hence what decision making is all about, in that it involves just such a communal discernment of the movement of the Spirit.

Before trying to explicate the problem more fully or suggesting a way in which the problem may be seen as providing a possibility for creative theology, it is appropriate to acknowledge that this problem is not everyone's problem. There are other ways of thinking about the New Testament as a source for literary interpretation or as a resource for theology.

Indeed, most people who take the Bible seriously and read it for guidance in their decisions care not in the least for scholarly lucubrations. They interpret the text creatively in all sorts of ways without even a side-glance concerning proper method of hermeneutical sophistication. So natural, long-standing, and pervasive is this untidy—indeed, unruly—conversation swirling about the Scripture that theologians might begin to learn from it some lessons. The first is modesty about our own efforts; we can observe the conversation and even have a small voice within it, but we cannot control it. The second is a change in attitude: All of this untidy, unmanageable discourse about and with the Bible need not be (as the educated are prone to think) perversity; it may be, indeed, the Spirit's preferred way of finding a space for its freedom.

The present discussion concerns theology and not popular religion. Theology is a small, highly specialized, but not necessarily well-defined fragment of a larger and more interesting conversation. People who do theology have at least this in common: They locate the *authority* of the text in its *being read*. Does this seem too obvious? Perhaps, but it makes a useful distinction from all those religious uses of the Bible which are fundamentally talismanic. Sometimes the talismanic use of the Bible is obvious, as when we swear on the book or incense it. Sometimes it is more subtle. Is it "theology" to extract a handful of verses, arrange them in a set of propositions, and apply them to every circumstance without ever actually *reading* them? In any case, I take it as axiomatic that theology in the proper sense is interested in the Bible as a text to be read and not as an object to venerate. How the Bible (and specifically the New Testament) is to be read, however, and how that reading is to function within the limited exercise called theology is not at all clear.

THEOLOGY AND THE INDIVIDUAL READER

In order to better understand why the literary diversity of the text is a particularly difficult problem for theologians today, a glance at previous readers may be helpful. Patristic theologians did not perceive the literary diversity of the New Testament as a great difficulty. To some extent we may wonder whether they perceived it at all. Certainly, disagreements between the evangelists on questions of fact concerning Jesus' ministry were attacked by educated opponents of Christianity such as Porphyry, requiring sustained rebuttal and the construction of Gospel harmonies. Certainly, theological differences between Paul and his opposition provided the occasion for theological discriminations such as that of Marcion. But these cavils were based not so much in specifically *literary* diversity as in the perception of historical or religious conflict. Sorting through such issues was the business of polemicists.

For the ordinary work of theology carried on in homilies, catechisms, edifying discourses, commentaries, letters, and disputations, the literary diversity of the New Testament writings scarcely was noticed. Yet, sophisticated readers like Origen knew and appreciated the conventions of their own literature, and could even acknowledge the presence of a genre, as Origen does when in his *Commentary on the Song of Songs* he calls it an epithalamium (a nuptial song). But this formal recognition has no real impact on his reading.

The general patristic neglect of the literary elements deriving from a human author's choices and intentions is rooted in a number of shared presuppositions concerning the source and nature of Scripture. Everyone agreed, for example, that the real and ultimate author of all the New Testament was the Holy Spirit; even when not explicitly stated, belief in divine inspiration was axiomatic. This conviction obviously relativized the significance of literary diversity and its corollary, authorial intention.

Belief in inspiration was accompanied and encouraged by an imaginative construal of the Scripture as a collection of divine oracles. Patristic writers took for granted that each verse of Scripture had its own revelatory value, was in effect much like an oracle delivered at Delphi, demanding yet enabling interpretation without reference to its immediate literary (literal) context. What appears to us as random proof-texting or a completely atomistic focus was not unprincipled. It was based on an appreciation of the Scripture as a collection of divine oracles *(logia)*, not as a collection of literary *compositions* whose message was communicated as a whole by means of intertextual signals.

A third shared premise was that the reading of these oracles was governed by the *regula fidei* and the teaching authority of the community. Irenaeus' greatness lay in his perception that the orthodox understanding of Scripture could stand against the wild vagaries of Gnostic interpretation only by steadily and equally maintaining the three legs of the canon of Scripture, the rule of faith, and the apostolic succession.

Irenaeus' own steadfast adherence to a literal-historical reading of both Testaments, however, had its own problems and was not universally followed. More frequently the ecclesial context provided a normative range of acceptable readings for those who preferred the more "spiritual" readings made available by allegory.

The sense of Scripture as a loose collection of oracles each of which could be independently interpreted was controlled by an ecclesial consensus (at least in fundamentals), resting on the synergy of bishop, canon, and creed. Yet the shared framework gave theologians great freedom in their reading of the text. Origen was the boldest, most imaginative orthodox theologian of all. But before he delved into his more arcane speculations, he patiently laid out the universally accepted elements of faith to which he also assented. He thereby felt himself free to build a system of readings erected on an anthropological analysis: The threefold meaning of Scripture at the literal-historical, moral, and allegorical levels corresponded to and was legitimated by the threefold constitution of humans as body, soul, and spirit.

Origen's allegorical approach came to dominate the theological appropriation of the New Testament. Its triumph was partly due to the historical fact that rival approaches (like Theodore of Mopsuestia's) were marginalized by heretical associations and geographical-cultural isolation. But the main reason for its victory was its admirable flexibility and comprehensiveness. If the deepest religious (theological) meaning of *every* text is to be found in its nonliteral, spiritual meaning, then the issue of literary diversity is bypassed entirely: The deep calls out to the deep, the spirit in the text speaks to the spirit in the reader.

Even the greatest admirers of Origen and of the allegorical approach must also recognize the costs of his victory. Theology in his mode is not only a highly intellectual and elitist activity (Origen sometimes has a hard time keeping his contempt for the "literalists" under control), it is also, in principle, private and individualistic. The framework of canon, church, and creed is indeed assumed and even affirmed, but it is not *engaged.* It is the individual reader's body, soul, and spirit that is addressed by the text, and addresses it in return. The church *as church* figures as an allegorical trope, but not as the reader nor as the one challenged to transformation. Allegory cannot build a community, cannot bring a community's experience into the process of reading, cannot—by the very nature of its method—have a reading *in common.* The more directly and individually the text is read, in fact, the more a communal sense of the text tends to disappear.

The consequence (as Reformation critics saw) was a distortion of both "scripture" and "tradition." The common life of the community could become progressively rote and rigid, because insufficiently challenged by the prophetic power of the scriptural texts. At the same time and for the same reason, the reading of the Scripture in sermon and commentary could become progressively random and fanciful. Allegorical readings could have great beauty and even power, but the connection between the reading and the text was sometimes difficult to detect. And as theology itself became purely scholastic, a scientific enterprise to be carried out by an individual scholar in the social context of the university, rather than by the preacher in the social context of the liturgical community, the patristic habit of proof-texting was carried even farther in elaborate collections of *loci communes* in support of dogmatic propositions.

The Reformation offered incisive criticism, but no solution. Indeed, by kicking out one leg of the tripod, that of the church, the principle of *sola scriptura* only made the theological appropriation of the New Testament more problematic. Yes, allegory was vigorously rejected in favor of the literal meaning. But allegory alone was not the problem! The basic *premise* of allegory, that the vivifying power of Scripture is to be found in the reading *by an individual* was if anything made even more explicit by the Reformation. The word of God spoke directly to the heart of the individual without mediation.

The principle of free interpretation based on the literal sense led directly if paradoxically to the remarkable fragmentation of Protestantism into thousands of disputing parties. Why? Because the literal sense is directed to the practical life of communities, not to the imagination or spirituality of individuals. The literal sense begs to be translated into action and practice and structure. But if each person is free (indeed obliged) to determine that literal sense as guided without intermediary by the Spirit, then division on the basis of different readings must quickly and inevitably follow. It seems impossible to combine a theology based on the literal sense, the principle of free individual interpretation, and a unified church.

Not that desperate measures to combine them have been lacking. Both the efforts of the Tübingen School and of the Biblical Theology movement can be seen as attempts to root theology in something "objective"—whether it be the reconstituted reality called "history," which in proper Hegelian style is itself regarded as the vehicle of theology—or some ineluctable quantity extracted from the text (though not exactly "in the text" either) that can gain universal assent, such as "Salvation History." The corrosive acid of post-modern criticism, however, has revealed how loosely glued these measures in fact always were. The more we seriously try to do "history," the less plausible appears its use for the distinct mode of knowing called theology.

The recent collapse of "Biblical Theology" in its classic form was the collapse of a sustained attempt to ground theological consensus on an objective understanding of the text without explicit appeal to the authority of church or creed. In the aftermath, we can observe a more general flight from every sort of authority except that of the individual reader. The authority of the community is absent, the authority of the creed is not determinative, and now even the authority of the text (as some sort of historically verifiable entity) is abandoned. What remains is the principle of free interpretation, rooted in the subjectivity of the individual reader. What remains, in other words, is chaos.

However fanciful the flights of Origen and his allegorical successors, and however much their individualistic readings eroded the sense of canon, church, and creed, they never explicitly abandoned them. There always existed, therefore, at least the possibility of conversation between various theologies and strategies of reading. The difference between Origen and today's proponents of reader-response theories is the deliberate abandonment of any coherent community code of conduct and convictions as a context, much less as a guide, to reading. As I understand the intellectual fashion called post-modernism (at least in its literary manifestation of deconstructionism), the collapse of all such normative and alienating structures of meaning is celebrated. The literary critic and the theologian use the text primarily as the occasion for self-referential reflection. The pertinence of the *literal* meaning for theology is the resistance it offers to subjective manipulation. But if the point of all reading is to celebrate such subjective manipulation, then the literal meaning is otiose.

I am indeed painting with a coarse-bristled brush! Please do not stumble over all these *obiter dicta*. I know as well as you how much they need qualification, debate, at least footnotes! But if I paused to support all these assertions, I would need a monograph, and would still not get to my own thesis. I therefore beg your indulgence for all these historical generalizations and too-tidy compartmentalizations. My purpose in these remarks has not been to disqualify any sort of reading or for that matter any mode of doing theology. It is possible, I am sure, to define theology in terms of an individual's thinking about God, or as an individual thinker's attempt to interpret the world in terms of faith in God. One could also on the basis of such a definition make a pretty fair argument that some contemporary literary criticism has as much of a religious and perhaps even theological character, as do the biblical interpretations of Origen, or the (also highly arbitrary) biblical construals of a Barth or a Bultmann.

My purpose instead has been to emphasize that for all the individualistic, subject-based strategies of reading, the literary diversity of the New Testament is no real problem, since the literal meaning itself is at best only a secondary consideration. But just the opposite is the case in the model of theology I will speak of next.

THEOLOGY AS THE ARTICULATION
OF THE FAITH OF THE CHURCH

Another way of defining theology—and the way I define it in this book—is as an ecclesial activity, as the articulation of the faith of the church. Since even this definition is capable of multiple understandings, some clarification is required. The most efficient procedure may be to focus on the separate terms.

By church, I mean not an organization but a living organism. I mean a local community gathered on the basis of the word of God and committed to Jesus as Lord. The first proper locus of theology is not the classroom but such a community. The life of this community requires explication, because it is there that the experience of God (everywhere else real but implicit) is brought to explicit expression. The main business of theology is not speculative and theoretical, but practical and prudential. It is to discern the word of God in the lives of humans. Pastoral theology is not the retail outlet for nuggets of truth about God refined in the crucible of philosophical analysis. If in fact theology has to do not alone with ideas but with faith in the living God, pastoral or practical theology is the research arm of theology.

By faith, then, I do not mean simply the framework of belief expressed by the creed, although the creed is part of the normative framework structuring the church's activity. The creed defines and offers inexhaustible possibilities for depth, but does not by itself enliven. Faith in the proper sense is rather the response of the human spirit to the call of God in the world, a response of belief, trust, obedience, and loyalty within the specific circumstances of worldly structures and activities. The subject of theology is the living God, who presses implicitly on us in our every encounter with the world. And since God's activity always precedes us (most fundamentally as the gift of creation renewed at every moment), theology must always be an open-ended, constantly changing response to that initiative.

Living faith seeks to understand the Living One to whom it responds. It thereby also seeks to understand itself and the implications of being so called and so gifted. So understood, theology is essentially an ecclesial activity. The theological task is implied by the very life of faith itself. Every Christian is called to seek an understanding of his or her response of faith, every Christian is called to the act of discernment of God's activity in the world and within the community. The church is not simply a set of symbols with reference to which a theologian works. The church is the place within which the activity called theology makes sense, as all the faithful seek articulation and understanding of their common life in the Spirit.

For this activity to take place, the work of God in the Spirit is presumed, is in fact the premise that generates theology in the first place: Human lives are intersected by the power and presence of God in the world. Furthermore, theology presumes that God's power and presence are truly *experienced* in the lives of humans, not always explicitly, clearly, or unambiguously, but truly. In defeat, depression, despair, and death as much as in triumph, success, hope, and healing are lives touched by the merciful and mighty One. But how can those diverse experiences be raised to the level of ecclesial discernment? Theology seeks to give voice to these implicit experiences through *narratives of faith*, which progressively reach toward a community narrative of God's work.

In the speaking and hearing of such narratives the community as such is addressed by the work of the Holy Spirit in the present instance, and is called to respond, is challenged afresh to a decision in favor of God's work, and thereby to a new interpretation of its life of faith. I am not by any means suggesting that the experience of God in the world is accessible for casual inspection. The process of discernment is difficult and filled with risk. The interpretation of the present moment in terms of God's activity is perilous and prone to error. It requires constant renewal and revision. But such discernment, such interpretation of God's word as speaking in and through the dispositions of human freedom, is the absolutely fundamental and necessary task of theology.

THE NORMATIVE ROLE OF SCRIPTURE

I am therefore defining theology first of all as a reading of the *texts of human lives* in a continuing process of self-revelation by the Living God, rather than as first of all a reading of the *texts of Scripture* as a record of a past and finished revelation. This raises the question of the normative role of the scripture generally, and for Christian theology in particular, of the New Testament. How do the scriptural texts function within this understanding of theology? Have they lost their normative authority, or are they seen to exercise it in a different way?

The ecclesial process of discerning and articulating God's word in contemporary life requires as an essential component the discernment and articulation of God's Word in the Scripture. The community does not regard the New Testament simply as an interesting if haphazard congeries of historical vignettes, or as a compelling anthology of literary insights, or as a classic collection of community customs. It acknowledges it as the canon of Scripture, and with that acknowledgment, confesses as well that in some fashion these texts have prophetic authority for the church in every age and place: They do not only have a meaning in the past, they have a significance for the present.

Implicit in the recognition of the New Testament as prophetic is the acknowledgment of these writings as "inspired by God." But in contrast to the ancient appreciation of divine inspiration, this ecclesial model for theology insists that the full implications of human authorship be taken into account in any reading. The confession of divine inspiration in other words is not a theory of literary composition, but an attribution of authority, not a reason to bypass consideration of literary structure and authorial intent but an invitation to do so.

Functionally, to speak of Scripture as inspired means that the church does not seek to subsume these texts into its own agenda, make them its own possession, reduce them to ideology. It means that these texts are regarded as "other," addressing the present circumstances of the community with the same voice (albeit in a different mode) as the narratives of the experience of God among the faithful. As the church discusses and debates and makes decisions pertinent to the meaning and the demands of God's kingdom for its own place and time, the texts of the New Testament provide the symbolic framework for the discernment of God's Word in the world, the language and perceptions that *enable* the church to discern the work of the Holy Spirit and distinguish it from the realm of the demonic and destructive.

But by themselves the texts of the New Testament do not exhaust the possibilities of God's action; rather, they are continually opened to new dimensions of meaning, constantly reinterpreted in light of the astonishing things God does in the world. By itself the experience of God in the community as expressed through narratives of faith is not a *norma non normata*, nor is the text of Scripture; both are essential moments in a dialectic of experience and interpretation that constantly characterizes the living faith community.

For the texts of the New Testament to exercise their authoritative functions within the community as part of a continuing process of theological reflection (to *author* identity according to the mind of Christ, to *authorize* modes of interpretation, and to provide *authorities* for the church's debate), it is necessary that they be engaged at the literal level. I recognize that the term "literal" is itself scarcely unequivocal, and can mean different things. At the most basic level I mean the text in its most publicly available form, the text as it comes to us most as "other," and as least shaped by our individual preconceptions and preconstruals. I mean the text as the mediator of ecclesial identity through the successive historical realizations of the church from its earliest times. In short, I mean the diverse compositions of the canon taken in all their literary diversity and historically conditioned symbols. It is in this form that the text can address the church as "other" than itself, and become part of a dialogical process involving many voices, instead of being another element in our individual or communal stream of consciousness.

We come at last to the precise problem presented to this understanding of the theological task by the literary diversity of the New Testament. On the one hand, the historically and linguistically conditioned meaning of the text is imperative for the New Testament to speak to us *as* other, and to be available to the discernment of all. And for the text to mediate the identity of an entire community, it can only be through the literal (functionally, the commonly available) reading of it. On the other hand, the very "otherness" of the text is fragmented and differentiated. The literary diversity of these writings seems to preclude the community's hearing any single voice it can heed and obey.

PROBLEM OR POSSIBILITY?

I have used the expression "untidy conversation" to characterize theology in the church. I suggest that the untidiness is cause not for dismay but for celebration, and that the problems presented by the literary diversity of the New Testament writings actually turn out to be openings to new possibilities. To see things this way requires something of a mental conversion, a letting go of certain idolatrous closures in order to embrace the freedom God offers us.

We must let go of any fantasy concerning the church as a stable, predictable, well-regulated organization. If the church is truly the place in the world where the experience of God is brought to the level of narrative and discernment, then the church will always be disorderly, a family living under stress, because it will as a community always be in transition between partial closure and openness, between the idolatry of institutional self-preservation and the obedience of faith in the living God. We must let go of the desire for theology to be a finished product of complete conceptual symmetry. If theology is in fact the attempt to understand living faith, then it must always be an unfinished process, for the data continues to come in, as the Living God persists in working through the lives of people and being revealed in their stories.

We must also let go of any pretense of closing the New Testament within some comprehensive, all-purpose, singular reading which reduces its complexity to simplicity. Whether we call it New Testament Theology, or Narrativity, or Existential Hermeneutics, or something else, we must recognize our attempts to reduce multiplicity to unity, to nail down some central, single, encompassing meaning in the New Testament that is also and above all portable, as attempts precisely at closure. We must recognize our tendency to seek a stable package of meaning that we can then apply to other situations or fit within our systematic theological constructs, so that, ideally, we need never really read the texts again.

A conversion to an understanding of church, theology, and the reading of Scripture which is appropriate to faith in the Living God is one that is fully committed (though never fully realized, because the inertia of idolatry always pulls us backward) to the risk-filled, tricky, and unpredictable freedom of the Spirit. We celebrate (with understandable trepidation) the fact that the church is inevitably and properly a community that is unstable, that must always make up its identity as it goes along, that is always experiencing conflict, because conflict is simply one of the faces of discernment in a community context. We rejoice (with some misgivings) in the fact that theology can never be packaged and distributed as a product, but must always remain a fragmented and fragile process, always trying to catch up with the One who constantly precedes our thought in action. We abandon (with considerable fear) the longing for a singular, fixed understanding of the New Testament that is not open to further revision, deepening, and extension, but recognize that its texts are a world in which we must continue to dwell, whose contours we must always reexamine each morning, whose faces are always changing, whose voices can still surprise.

By no means, however, are we thereby cast adrift in formless subjectivism. It is as a *community* that we commit ourselves to these perceptions, and as a community we are bound by any number of constraints that govern and give shape to the messy project of interpreting faith in the Living God. And if we are a real community that meets together, and not simply an abstraction called church, then our search for meaning is not absolutely and dangerously free-floating. We share the life of a historical community with specific traditions of belief and behavior and with specific instruments and procedures for making decisions and exercising authority. Our identities are shaped by our patterns of worship and the use of Scripture within worship and sacrament. Our discernment of God's word in the narratives of faith enunciated within the assembly is guided by the rule of faith that we share as part of our heritage. The texts we engage as part of our communal conversation about the nature and demands of God's activity among us are finite. As the canon of Scripture, they are also part of the tradition handed down to us. We have more than enough structure to allow some spontaneity.

It is an essential aspect of the church's historical tradition, in fact, that the canon is made up of discrete literary compositions. Too seldom has theology appreciated this remarkable fact. The process and ratification of the canon over the first three centuries institutionalized the literary diversity of Christian Scripture. The temptation offered by Tatian to replace the messiness of four separate Gospels with a single, coherent, harmonized life of Jesus was rejected. The temptation offered by Marcion to reject theological plurality in favor of a (simplified) Paulinism was even more emphatically rejected. Nor was anyone ever terribly concerned about what happened to the authority of the New Testament in translation; versions proliferated merrily and without hesitation because of the conviction (implicit to be sure) that in the New Testament God's word was to be found not in the life of Jesus or in a theology or in the transformative power of the Greek language, but *in and through the diverse literary compositions as such*.

Our appreciation for the literary and rhetorical diversity of the New Testament could not, then, be more in tune with the implicit logic of the canonizers. In this respect, not Origen with his construal of Scripture as a set of *logia* inspired by God, but we with our construal of the canon as a collection of compositions written by human authors, are closer to the tradition that shapes authentic Christian identity. It is *as* self-contained literary compositions, each with its own internal integrity, that the writings *most resist* our manipulation, and therefore most challenge our individual and communal preconceptions.

But we are also obliged to deal more explicitly with the full implications of this literary diversity. The more we study the Gospels in literary terms, for example, the more we become aware how profoundly their message, their "voice" is embedded in their overall literary structure. No one schooled in the literary analysis of the Gospels could assert that Mark and Matthew were really "saying the same thing." Likewise the more we take seriously the multiple rhetorical conventions operative in the epistolary literature, the less willing we are to think of Galatians and Romans as "basically making the same point." Still less are we willing to talk about the "teaching of the Synoptic Gospels," or the "theology of Paul," and quite rightly, for we are aware that by seeking such systematization, we lose more than we gain, we lose precisely the nature and quality of the voice enunciated by each of these compositions.

We are coming to appreciate with specific and detailed clarity how each New Testament composition speaks, not as the repository of early sources or of historical data, not as a set of truthful propositions about the reality of God and the world, but as a coherent, intricately and intentionally contrived literary composition, whose structure and rhetoric are not a disposable surface effect but the very vehicle of meaning. The failure to produce a really convincing theology of the New Testament in recent years may in fact derive in part from the implicit recognition that reducing literary multiplicity to theological unity comes at too great a cost.

But how difficult, it would seem, to deal theologically with this literary diversity! No progress will be made, however, if we think that the answer lies in creating smaller portable packets, such as "the theology of Luke-Acts" or "the theology of Mark," for if these are smaller abstractions, they are still abstractions. But then how arduous, trying to work our way through all the hurdles to quick and easy appropriation posed by an entire literary composition. What part of it do we focus on? Whose reading do we accept? Must we become experts in literary criticism in order to be theologians? Don't we find ourselves in a hopeless regressive debate over the meaning of the text without ever getting to the task of theology? These are the questions of people who think of theology as an academic discipline. And if we think of theology as an academic enterprise, then yes, the issues become hopelessly entangled. Then the direct appropriation of the New Testament in its literary diversity would be endlessly arduous, complex, confusing.

But what if we think of theology first of all as an ecclesial process of discernment? Then it is the most natural thing in the world to read through an entire Gospel together as a community, paying the closest attention to the way it elicits our own narratives of faith, challenges our own words, as it unfolds in its literary integrity. Will there be many and even conflicting readings? Of course there will be, as many as there are members of the church taking part. And are these multiple readings a problem? No, because they are not essays in a book on hermeneutics, or academic contributions to the science of reading, but are all part of a fluid, continuing, dialogical, open process of discernment, rooted in and guided by the Gospel itself, not as an abstraction but as a voice that speaks to each one of us and to us all with power. The same is, if anything, even more true of reading Paul's Letters, or the book of Revelation, or the other epistolary literature of the New Testament.

Only within this *communal* process of reading and discernment, in fact, do these writings come to life as they were intended to from the beginning. The writings of the New Testament were not composed for private readership, after all, or for individual interpretation. They were composed as documents written for *communities*. They were intended to be read aloud, and to be interpreted in preaching, and to be open to the discernment of all. They are therefore best fitted not to the transformation of individual lives, but to the edification of communities. This is why they were written and is the work they do best.

In the give-and-take of communal reading and interpretation, the texts of the New Testament are encountered as they were meant to be encountered. The dangers of subjectivity and distortion are reduced, for the process of discernment is open and public. The voice of each writing is heard in its own terms with minimal manipulation exercised by excerpting or packaging. The literal meaning of the text is finally freed for its work within a community for the building up of that community's identity and holiness. And as the community reads different texts from the New Testament, it begins to learn that these many voices help to shape many legitimate ways of living out that identity, that within the broad consensus of community commitment, a healthy diversity of life is actually authorized by the New Testament itself. It may begin to learn as well the ways in which the New Testament does not speak directly or explicitly to its situation, but must be cracked open by the experience and insights gained by the Spirit's working in the church.

I am suggesting that the irreducible literary diversity of the New Testament canon resists the efforts of the academician-theologian to systematize and thereby ossify the texts, but that this same literary diversity opens itself to the doing of theology within the community of faith as an essential part of the discernment of God's Word in the world. Is this cause for dismay? Only if we think that being a librarian is more important than reading books, or being a grammarian more significant than writing poetry.

PART TWO

EXEGESIS

CHAPTER 4

DIFFICULTIES

If my sketch of the task of theology and of ecclesial hermeneutics makes sense, then we can begin the process of listening to the voices of Scripture. We do not expect to find a single, univocal testimony, nor are we dismayed at the prospect of hearing many and perhaps discordant voices. At this point, we are not even sure what questions to ask the voices, or which ones we should perhaps pay more attention to. We suspect that the questions, and the sense of how to listen, might itself involve a dialectic process between our minds and the texts themselves. We begin with a vague question that we bring to the texts, but we are open to being instructed by the texts in what the questions more properly might be.

We begin, then, by looking for scriptural passages that can address the church's ways of reaching decision as a group. We need passages speaking of the church as a group, not just as individuals within the group, and speaking of decision making as a human process, not simply as a reported event, or one caused only by God. These criteria effectively narrow the search to the New Testament. The obvious reason is that the church as such is not found in the Old Testament. And even those passages that may contain suggestions of future developments (Moses' appointment of the seventy elders in Exod. 18:13-17, or his desire that all Israelites should be prophets, in Num. 11:24-30) are placed within contexts that do not provide useful analogies. For this particular discussion—it may be different for other issues—the New Testament witnesses address the church's practice and self-understanding more directly.

Even within the New Testament, there are a limited number of texts that appear as obviously pertinent. Fewer still are extensive. Most of the passages about decision making are fragmentary, in the sense that they come at the issue only partially or indirectly. A group of narrative texts, on the other hand, displays the decision-making process rather fully. The fragmentary texts, because they are in the form of exhortations and directives, are more easily regarded as theologically pertinent. The narratives do not appear to yield any norms.

Two separate interpretative difficulties face the reader from the beginning. The first concerns the relative importance to be given to the witnesses. Indiscriminate harmonizing is always bad method. In this case, however, there is something to be said for viewing the fragmentary texts as complementing the fuller ones, so long as this procedure does not detract from their own distinctive voice. I will first survey these partial and scattered references to see how they might fit within a more complete picture. But then, a second and more difficult question needs to be faced: How can narrative passages be read as vehicles for theological reflection?

SOME SCATTERED WITNESSES

The place we would most like to find texts concerning decision making is the Letters of Paul. The reasons for this are twofold. First, because Paul's focus is always fixed on the life of the local assembly. Apart from Ephesians, Paul's references to church signify the people called together by God in a particular locality. Second, because Paul always seeks to delineate the theological implications of the church's common activity.

Unfortunately, there is relatively little in Paul directly applicable to this issue, although what he does say fits well within the fuller picture we have yet to develop on the basis of narrative texts. Despite the fact that Paul constantly issues apostolic instructions and exhortations that demand decisions of his communities, his letters rarely show us how the community might go about reaching such decisions. This lack might be attributable to Paul's claim of personal apostolic authority over his churches and his extraordinary involvement in their life. But since the other New Testament epistolary literature contains even less information than Paul on this subject, it may only be that procedures for reaching decision were sufficiently practiced and understood to require little underscoring.

It is clear, for example, that Paul recognizes the presence of local authority structures in his communities (see Rom. 12:8; 1 Cor. 6:1-6; 12:4-11; 16:15-18; Gal. 6:6; Eph. 4:11; Phil. 1:1; 1 Thess. 5:12). And his letters do contain some instructions concerning actions and attitudes relevant to the process of reaching decision in the church. In 1 Timothy 5:1-24, for example, Paul not only directs his delegate on the proper attitude he should have toward diverse members of the church (5:1-2) and sets guidelines for the treatment of widows (5:3-16), but demands that certain procedures be followed when local leaders are accused of wrongdoing by others in the community. He insists that no charge be admitted except on the evidence of two or three witnesses (5:19). This practice not only recalls the norm set in Deuteronomy 19:15—an example of using the Scripture to validate the church's practice—but it also shows us the involvement of more than the interested parties in a dispute which affects the well-being of the group as a whole. Paul insists above all that prejudice and partiality are to be avoided in settling such complaints (5:21). The passage also suggests the difficulty of making some determinations concerning behavior in the community, requiring the passage of time for the real story to emerge: "The sins of some [people] are conspicuous, pointing to judgment, but the sins of others appear later" (5:24). Apart from the presence of the witnesses, however, we do not see the assembly as such involved here. It is Paul's delegate who is to carry out these instructions.

It is characteristic of Paul, in fact, to stress individual responsibility for making decisions, even when the greater good of the community is at stake. Note, for example, the delicacy of Galatians 6:1-5: Mutual correction is a community responsibility, but it must always be tempered by gentleness, by an awareness of one's own frailty, and by the necessity of testing one's own work. In his treatment of the unrest caused by different observances in the church of Rome, Paul similarly insists that all will have to answer to God for their own way of life (Rom. 14:4, 12), and rejects any notion that individuals within the church can judge the life of others (14:4, 10). He desires the mutual acceptance of legitimate differences within the church (14:13-14; 15:7). Each person must discern and decide what is best for himself or herself (14:5). At the same time, however, each person also has the responsibility of acting in a way which builds up the community in faith (14:19; cf. also Phil. 2:4).

His approach is virtually identical in 1 Corinthians in the discussion of eating meat offered to idols (8–10). Again he emphasizes the obligation to obey one's own conscience in such matters (1 Cor. 10:27-29), and the need for mutual edification (1 Cor. 8:12-13); but he does not suggest that the general issue, "Should Corinthian Christians eat meat offered to idols?" be decided by that church as a whole.

Paul's emphasis on individual discernment and decision is derived from his conviction concerning the spiritual nature of the Christian group. Not only charismatic leaders, but all believers have received the Holy Spirit (1 Cor. 12:13). Because of this, all in the community have been called to freedom (Gal. 5:13) and enjoy the freedom of God's children (Gal. 4:1-7), having been released from fear (Rom. 8:14-17). The Spirit provides the power for a new way of existence. It is also the power which enables Christians to interpret that existence (1 Cor. 2:12) and make choices consistent with it. So Paul tells the Galatians, "If we live by the Spirit, let us also walk by the Spirit" (Gal. 5:25). Each Christian, therefore, is capable, and therefore required, to interpret his or her life before God in the concrete choices demanded by worldly existence.

Paul by no means suggests that this is an automatic or easy process. But the transforming power of the Spirit enables people to "prove [or "test"] what is the will of God, what is good and acceptable and perfect" (Rom. 12:2). The testing process, moreover, is not entirely individualistic. It is true that Paul can say in Galatians 6:4, "Let each one test his own work," but he prepares for that statement by one coming just before it, "If a man is overtaken in any trespass, you who are spiritual should restore him in a spirit of gentleness" (Gal. 6:1; cf. also Col. 3:13). The exhortation implies some degree of communal discernment and correction, like that found in the command of James 5:19-20.

The church's responsibility for discerning the diverse movements of the Spirit within it is stated directly in 1 Thessalonians 5:19-22: "Do not quench the Spirit, do not despise prophesying, but test everything; hold fast what is good, abstain from every form of evil." In the Greek, these are all plural imperatives. The testing process is one required of the church as a group. This passage has some similarity to one outside the Pauline writings. In 1 John 4:1, we read, "Test the spirits to see whether they are of God; for many false prophets have gone out into the world." This passage deals with the problem of sorting out competing claims to spiritual authority and leadership. In Paul, the testing is done on the sort of behavior the Spirit appears to motivate, especially in prophecy. In both passages, the community as such is told to test, but in neither case is it told how to test. We will return to 1 Corinthians in chapter 6, to see whether Paul offers us in his discussion of tongues and prophecy in 1 Corinthians 12–14 some clues concerning criteria for testing the work of the Holy Spirit in the community.

The references we have just inventoried are scattered, but cumulatively they point to the realization that, even in a spiritual community, the impulses of the Spirit are not always obvious and may even be counterfeited. There is need for constant discernment. We have nowhere seen any indication that the church should judge an individual member. The emphasis, rather, has been on the judgment each must face before God. The discernment demanded of individuals, however, clearly takes place in a spiritual community which as a group of people bears some responsibility for the articulation of the Spirit's life within it, for it has been told, "Test every spirit."

SOME FULLER TESTIMONIES

When the discernment process is not being carried out by individuals, their choices can threaten to falsify the community's identity. The members may claim to live by the Spirit, but their actions betray the Spirit's authentic expression. When this happens, it becomes necessary for the church to exercise a more drastic sort of group discernment, if it is to retain its own integrity.

We find one example in 1 Corinthians 5:1-5. The passage is short but raises a number of problems. Whatever the precise nature of the man's offense it is clear that this member of the Corinthian congregation had overstepped the bounds of acceptable diversity and had fallen into dangerous deviance. Here it is not a question of legitimate freedom possibly causing offense, as with eating meat offered to idols. When a Christian behaves openly in the church in a manner offensive even to pagans (1 Cor. 5:1), with no objection being made by the community, the identity of the church as a people set apart by God for sanctification (1:2) is called into question. The boundary between "the saints" and "the world" (5:9-10) has collapsed, and the church has lost its distinctive witness. The body no longer symbolizes the spirit.

The situation in Corinth is exacerbated by the arrogance of the community (5:2), which leads it to judge between its teachers (1:12; 3:4), but not attend to the sort of discernment required if it is to remain God's church. Paul insists that the community recognize and reaffirm its true identity. It must come together as the church to deal with this issue (5:4-5).

Paul by no means leaves the decision up to them, however. Perhaps he thinks they had shown little capacity to use discernment. Instead, as one who is their father (4:15), an apostle (9:1) who certifiably has the Spirit of God (7:40), he directs them to hand over the offender to Satan (5:5). This is a ritual of some obscurity, but is clearly a form of excommunication. When the community gathers, it is in the name of the Lord Jesus, and although Paul is absent in body, he is present with them in spirit at the assembly (5:3). The excommunication is intended to work for the man's ultimate salvation (5:5). For the community, however, this ritual exclusion serves the purpose of reasserting its identity as the temple of God where the Spirit dwells (see 3:16), and therefore as a purification (see 5:6-7).

Paul supports the excommunication by appeal to Scripture: "Drive out the wicked person from among you" (Deut. 17:7), cited from the Greek translation (the Septuagint = LXX) in 1 Corinthians 5:13. Because the Christian community continues the story of God's people, earlier parts of the story provide norms for its own communal life (cf. also 1 Cor. 10:1-11; Rom. 15:4). Paul does not use the Deuteronomy passage mechanically. It had dealt with the evil of idolatry among the people Israel, and advocated the death of the offender. By applying this passage to a sexual offense, which was to be punished by excommunication, Paul extends the meaning of the earlier passage. By so doing, of course, he also reinterprets it.

The extreme case of excommunication shows how Paul saw the need for the church to exercise discernment concerning its own life: "Is it not those inside the church whom you are to judge?" (1 Cor. 5:12). Only because the Corinthian church failed in this decision-making process has Paul stepped in from outside to save and chasten the community, and to reassert his legitimate authority over it. It is not certain, but highly likely, that we find another reference to this excommunication in 2 Corinthians 2:5-11. Paul refers to a "punishment by the majority" which was carried out (2 Cor. 2:6), and which he had insisted on to test them and see if they were obedient (2:9). And, as in 1 Corinthians 5:5, Satan is viewed as standing just outside the church's boundaries (2 Cor. 2:11). Paul recommends that the one punished now be forgiven, comforted, and regarded with love (2:7-8). The church which exercises discipline as a group is also capable, as a group, of forgiving and restoring to communion. The attitude Paul here recommends corresponds to that found in Galatians 6:1 and Colossians 3:13.

The problem of discipline and excommunication is also addressed in Matthew 18:15-20, a passage which appears to prescribe disciplinary practice for a particular community. Two of Matthew's three uses of the term "church" *(ekklēsia)* occur in this short passage (Matt. 18:17; see also 16:18). Here it is not a case of deviant behavior threatening the spiritual integrity of the church, but a process of correction running afoul. An individual member of the church done harm by another is told to deal with the problem personally by confronting the offender (18:15). But what if this does not work? "If he refuses to listen," then the church's intervention and decision are required (18:17). We see how the community is called upon to decide when the personal process fails. The church does not decide all cases, but decides the cases which affect all.

Matthew has Jesus propose an intermediate step in the two or three witnesses who accompany the offended party and try to resolve the matter with the offender (18:16). These represent the larger community. At least implicit reference is here made to the Scripture as warrant for the church's practice, for the use of two or three witnesses recalls Deuteronomy 19:15 (as it did in 1 Tim. 5:19). The process moves in stages from the individual to the communal.

Only if the offender does not heed these witnesses is the story told to the assembly as a whole. For the first time in these fragmentary texts, we see the function of *narrative* in the decision-making process. The narration (by the offended person? by the witnesses?) forms the basis for the community discernment and decision (Matt. 18:17). If the offender listens, the health of the church's processes is affirmed. But what if the offender does not listen to the voice even of the church as a whole? Then the offender poses a direct threat to the community's right to reach decision. Such a frontal attack on the church's authority to decide its future and discipline its members can only be met with excommunication, for the survival of the group is at stake. Failed discipline leads logically to exclusion: "Let him be to you as a Gentile and a tax collector" (18:17). As in the case of the Corinthian excommunication, the assembly is gathered in the name of Jesus and has the power of Jesus present to it (18:20). For this reason, when the community reaches "agreement" (18:19), its decisions are "binding" with God (18:18).

Neither the Pauline nor the Matthean passage directly addresses the question, How should the church go about making decision? But from the specific cases of deviance and defiance leading to excommunication, we can deduce some of the implied norms of these communities, which are made explicit by the decision-making process. The assembly is clearly more than a collection of like-minded folk. When it is gathered in Jesus' name, the assembly is visited by the power of the Lord—the Holy Spirit. The church meets not to replace individual discernment, which is the responsibility of each member, but to address challenges posed to the group's life as a whole, challenges only the group can meet. The reaching of decision requires the assertion of the community's identity. It may call for the invocation, and therefore rereading, of Scripture.

There is a final narrative fragment from Paul's Letter to the Galatians that demands our attention, while providing a transition to those fuller narrative passages whose peculiar problems we must next trace. The narrative in this case is highly charged, serving at once as a defense of Paul's practice, and as an example to the Galatians as to how they should also stand by their experience of freedom in the Holy Spirit and resist those who would bring them under a strict construal of Torah. In Galatians 2:1-10, Paul reports a decision reached by him and the leaders of the Jerusalem church—James, Cephas, John. The agreement was sealed by "the right hand of fellowship" between Paul and Barnabas on one side, and the Jerusalem leaders on the other (Gal. 2:9). The Jerusalem leaders agreed on the legitimacy of Paul's preaching to Gentiles, and on the inclusion of Gentiles in the church. They recognized that in both Peter's ministry to the circumcised and Paul's to the uncircumcised, God had been at work (2:8). In deciding for the inclusion of the Gentiles, therefore, they decided for God. The Jewish Christian leaders recognized that the mission of Paul and Barnabas resulted from a grace given by God (2:9).

Most remarkable in this short report is the basis for the decision. Paul says he went up because of a vision, and "I laid before them (but privately before those who were of repute) the gospel which I preach among the Gentiles" (2:2). The Greek verb "lay before" *(anatithēmi)* has the sense of "submit," but also (as in Acts 25:14) the sense of "relate, communicate." It is precisely Paul's *narration,* his telling of what he did and taught among the Gentiles, which allowed the other leaders to discern that this was God's work.

The human elements of the story are all too evident. The polemic, however, cannot hide a process of decision making in the church of the first generation that made conscious acknowledgment of the transcendent context for its life (Gal. 2:2, 6, 8, 9), which allowed for a challenge potentially threatening to the group to be expressed in a narrative of faith (2:2), and which led to decision on the basis of discerning God's work active in the lives of others.

AN EXTENDED NARRATIVE: ACTS 15:1-35

This passage takes up virtually an entire chapter in the Acts of the Apostles, the second volume of the work often referred to as Luke-Acts. It narrates a critical event in the life of the early church, sometimes called the Apostolic Council. This account, as we shall see later, is itself the climax to a series of earlier passages in Acts that are pertinent to our discussion. Even considered in isolation, it is unique in the New Testament for the fullness of the attention it gives to the decision-making process. The problems it presents for theological appropriation have to do with its character as a *narrative*. Since this passage will occupy so much of our attention, I will present it in full according to the RSV translation.

> But some men came down from Judea and were teaching the brethren, "Unless you are circumcised according to the custom of Moses, you cannot be saved." And when Paul and Barnabas had no small dissension and debate with them, Paul and Barnabas and some of the others were appointed to go up to Jerusalem to the apostles and the elders about this question. So, being sent on their way by the church, they passed through both Phoenicia and Samaria, reporting the conversation of the Gentiles, and they gave great joy to all the brethren. When they came to Jerusalem, they were welcomed by the church and the apostles and the elders, and they declared all that God had done with them. But some believers who belonged to the party of the Pharisees rose up, and said, "It is necessary to circumcise them, and to charge them to keep the law of Moses."
>
> The apostles and the elders were gathered together to consider this matter. And after there had been much debate, Peter rose and said to them, "Brethren, you know that in the early days God made choice among you, that by my mouth the Gentiles should hear the word of the gospel and believe. And God who knows the heart bore witness to them, giving them the Holy Spirit just as he did to us; and he made no distinction between us and them, but cleansed their hearts by faith. Now therefore why do you make trial of God by putting a yoke upon the neck of the disciples which neither our fathers nor we have been able to bear? But we believe that we shall be saved through the grace of the Lord Jesus, just as they will."
>
> And all the assembly kept silence; and they listened to Barnabas and Paul as they related what signs and wonders God had done through them among the Gentiles. After they finished speaking, James replied, "Brethren, listen to me. Simeon has related how God first visited the Gentiles, to take out of them a people for his name. And with this the words of the prophets agree, as it is written, 'After this I will return, / and I will rebuild the dwelling of David, which has fallen; / I will rebuild its ruins, / and I will set it up, / that the rest of men may seek the Lord, / and all the Gentiles who are called by my name, / says the Lord, who has made these things known from of old.' Therefore my judgment is that we should not trouble those of the Gentiles who turn to God, but should write to them to abstain from the pollutions of idols and from unchastity and from what is strangled and from blood. For from early generations Moses has had in every city those who preach him, for he is read every sabbath in the synagogues."
>
> Then it seemed good to the apostles and the elders, with the whole church, to choose men from among them and send them to Antioch with Paul and Barnabas. They sent Judas called Barsabbas, and Silas, leading

men among the brethren, with the following letter: "The brethren, both the apostles and the elders, to the brethren who are of the Gentiles in Antioch and Syria and Cilicia, greeting. Since we have heard that some persons from us have troubled you with words, unsettling your minds, although we gave them no instructions, it has seemed good to us, having come to one accord, to choose men and send them to you with our beloved Barnabas and Paul, men who have risked their lives for the sake of our Lord Jesus Christ. We have therefore sent Judas and Silas, who themselves will tell you the same things by word of mouth. For it has seemed good to the Holy Spirit and to us to lay upon you no greater burden than these necessary things: that you abstain from what has been sacrificed to idols and from blood and from what is strangled and from unchastity. If you keep yourselves from these, you will do well. Farewell."

So when they were sent off, they went down to Antioch; and having gathered the congregation together, they delivered the letter. And when they read it, they rejoiced at the exhortation. And Judas and Silas, who were themselves prophets, exhorted the brethren with many words and strengthened them. And after they had spent some time, they were sent off in peace by the brethren to those who had sent them. But Paul and Barnabas remained in Antioch, teaching and preaching the word of the Lord, with many others also.

SCHOLARSHIP ON ACTS 15

Given the generally overgrown state of New Testament scholarship, one might suppose that the possible pertinence of Acts 15 to anything would have been noticed by now, and certainly its relevance to the process by which the church reaches its decisions. But a survey of what has been written on the passage over the past several decades shows a remarkably narrow range of interest in it.

Among those working within the guild of New Testament scholarship, the passage has been studied from the point of view of several "criticisms." The text-critical question has stirred some interest, because of the characteristic and extensive variants (Codex D at 15:20 and 15:29 inserts the "Golden Rule" among the other parts of the decree). Others have asked the source-critical question: What, if anything, in this passage goes back to previous sources, and how has the final editor reworked them? The greatest amount of attention has been given to the historical-critical question, namely the relation between this passage and Galatians 2, which, as we have seen, also reports a meeting between Paul and the Jerusalem leaders, but in quite a different manner. The historical issues of chronology, accuracy, and bias are raised by the apparent conflict, if not contradiction, between the two reports.

In particular, the reality or fate of the so-called apostolic decree (Acts

15:23-29) has proved to be a knotty problem. If there really was such a decree, why didn't Paul, in his discussion of meats offered to idols in 1 Corinthians 8–10, refer to it? Was he actually in disagreement with it? Or did the decree have only a regional application (in Antioch, Syria, and Cilicia according to Acts 15:23) and not necessarily apply in Corinth? Was there a decree at all, or did Luke make it up? Some attention has also been given to the thematic role played by James's discourse in 15:14-21, as well as to the influence this narrative had in the formation of the "conciliar idea" in early Christianity. That these historical questions have preoccupied New Testament scholars is neither particularly surprising nor reprehensible. Until very recently New Testament scholarship thought of itself as basically a historical enterprise.

It is a bit more surprising to discover the neglect of Acts 15 in theological works devoted expressly to the church. Especially in an era when "world" and "ecumenical" councils have generated so much theological reflection, Acts 15 would seem the perfect text to exploit as a paradigm. There is no end to what is written, of course, and I may have missed even significant contributions, but my own reading in the area has not yielded any serious appropriation of Acts 15 by theological discussion. The references I have found tend to be casual and somewhat *pro forma*, even in writings specifically dealing with the conciliar ideal. Why haven't theologians used this passage?

Doctrinal theologians try to work with biblical material as mediated to them by biblical scholars. The constantly changing face of biblical scholarship has created the impression, even among theologians, that only those professionally trained in that field can possibly excavate the texts of the Bible. New Testament scholars, in turn, have been using the historical-critical method in their investigations. Historical methods can ask only historical questions, which can receive only historical answers. Consequently, the data supplied theologians by biblical scholars has tended to take the form of historical information. In theological works on the church, for example, we find that Acts is used as a source of information about the forms of ministry in the early church, but it appears to offer little else for theological reflection.

The dominance of the historical method has had a powerful effect on the theological appropriation of biblical texts. Some unspoken assumptions exercise considerable influence. One of these is that "history" is itself the vehicle of theology, so that the historical form of the early church has critical theological relevance for the church today—if we can but reconstruct it. Another assumption is that the methods of historical inquiry can function as theological criteria. We can see this assumption at work when theologians use the conclusions of historians on the dating, authorship, and authenticity of New Testament writings as norms for their theology and worth. Luke-Acts, for example, is conventionally regarded as a writing coming from the second Christian generation. Since that generation is seen as one in which the earliest "charismatic" structure of the church had become routinized and institutionalized, Luke-Acts must therefore be reading back into its account of the first generation the perceptions of a later generation. His portrait of the church, therefore, "must" be one in which the Spirit is demoted and tradition has replaced enthusiasm; the picture of the church in Luke-Acts "must" betray the picture of the church in Paul. There is little in either Paul's Letters or Luke-Acts to support these opinions, however widely they are held. What is remarkable, however, is that they are not only held by scholars doing history, but by those doing theology as well.

Acts 15 has also been studied from the viewpoint of biblical theology, especially as found in works on the church in the New Testament. The intention to do theology in biblical terms is laudable, but in practice, biblical theology has often been little more than an archaeological dig. The result has been that the biblical witness remains firmly in the past, even farther removed from our theological appropriation. Insofar as "New Testament theology," for example, has attempted to establish some unity among the obviously diverse New Testament writings, it has done so at the cost either of harmonizing them, or of selecting some as more normative than others. Both moves betray the canonical principle, which asserts the normative importance of all the witnesses precisely in their diversity. Furthermore, the attempt to describe a "biblical worldview" in general or in particular topics has only accentuated the distance between that world and ours, for it has led to the impression that each is a fixed and separate "thing." Finally, much of what is done from this perspective amounts to a series of "theologies of": the "theology of Paul" or the "theology of Luke." This sort of descriptive appreciation is not yet theology.

The chapter given to Luke-Acts in New Testament studies of the church (ecclesiologies) concentrates on the Lucan notions of ministry. These notions are accounted for by the supposed historical situation and, therefore, the Lucan theological perceptions. In short, whether in technical New Testament scholarship, or in doctrinal or biblical theology, Acts 15 has been appropriated through the categories of history: the history of the text—with Luke as source; the history of ideas—with Luke the thinker studied.

THE HISTORICAL DIFFICULTY

Another aspect of this historical fixation is a preoccupation with what Luke says to the neglect of how he says it. Information yielded by the narrative is considered important; the shape of the narrative is not. The failure to read Acts 15 as a narrative with theological implications does not result from discrimination against this passage alone. It comes from a long-standing and pervasive neglect of biblical narratives both in Scripture studies and in theology. Recently, "literary" approaches to the New Testament appear to be reversing the trend. Such studies, however, have devoted far more attention to the aesthetic than to the theological dimensions of New Testament compositions. Few bridges have been thrown across the gap separating the realm of narrative from the realm of theological reflection, and none in the case of Acts 15.

But let us suppose a theologian wants to use the narrative of Acts 15 as a source for theological reflection on the church. Isn't the attempt futile, given the doubtful historicity of the story, and its apparent tendentiousness? In other words, if the story is not historically accurate, does it have any value for the church—as a historical community—in its process of seeking to understand itself and the one who calls it? We find ourselves at a critical juncture. If the theological use of a narrative text depends on its historical accuracy, we limit the narrative's range of meaning to the referential. It is the action of the past we consider meaningful; the narrative has worth only insofar as it accurately reports that event. Or perhaps it has some derivative interest as witness to the author's perception of the event. In either case, historicity becomes the touchstone of narrative worth.

The question of historicity is something of a false issue in the case of the Apostolic Council, anyway. Only the most intransigent skeptic would deny that behind the different and sometimes conflicting reports of Luke (Acts 15) and Paul (Galatians 2) there was a real and significant series of events. The discrepancies in the two sources are of interest, after all, only because of their general agreement. Something happened. Very early on in the life of the church there was a crisis stimulated by the conversion of non-Jews to belief in Jesus as Messiah and Lord. Gentiles, entering a community which till then had seen itself as the faithful remnant of God's people Israel, posed a challenge to the church's self-understanding. The church had to decide on the legitimacy of this Gentile mission. If that be granted, it had to decide what conditions would be required of them to be considered part of the people. The question came down to whether there would be one or two forms of Christianity.

To settle the matter, at least one meeting was held in Jerusalem—acknowledged by all participants as the mother church—where these issues were raised and discussed. Peter, Paul, James, and Barnabas all certainly took an active and important part. They reached a decision amicably. They remained in fellowship. Both sources regard the decision as having fundamental and far-reaching consequences.

Questions, of course, remain. Was there only one meeting, or more than one? Do the sources refer to the same or different meetings? Did Paul go to Jerusalem as part of an Antiochian delegation (Acts), or in response to personal revelation (Galatians)? Did Titus accompany Paul (Galatians), or not? Did this meeting precede or follow the stormy encounter between Paul and Cephas at Antioch where table fellowship was also the issue? Acts makes a conflict at Antioch the cause of the Council. But Paul locates the conflict with "certain men from James" and Cephas after the Jerusalem meeting. Was the decision of the leaders formulated in a "decree" (Acts)? Was part of the agreement that Paul and Barnabas should take up a collection (Galatians)? These are legitimate issues and remain grounds for further investigation. But by the standards of sane historiography, there is much more here that is certain than uncertain.

Then what about Luke's narrative? There are two main options. The first is that things happened the way he says they did, and he accurately records them. A corollary of this is that Paul is either talking about another meeting, or, deliberately or not, giving a mistaken account. High regard for Paul should not automatically rule out the possibility of his being slightly tendentious, as well. In this first option, Luke's account and history would coincide. The second option is that things happened quite differently from the way Luke describes them, that is, either as Paul has it, or in a manner altogether different from both sources. Luke, however, reports them the way he does for one of three reasons: (1) His sources are deficient or wrong; (2) he wishes to correct another version he regards as erroneous or one-sided; (3) consciously or not, he wishes to idealize the event, in order to teach the church. In this option, Luke writes with less concern for "what actually happened" than for "what should have happened."

For the sake of argument, let us take the third option as the most likely: Deliberately or not, Luke idealized the event. We are, in other words, at the farthest remove from what is usually regarded as accurate historical reporting. If our theological reflection depends on the absolute historical accuracy of the narrative, we can go no farther. Although Luke reports "something" that happened, the way he tells it distorts the event, and his narrative in its details, therefore, is useless. But another attitude toward Luke's narrative is possible. We can regard Luke as a divinely inspired teacher of the church, through whose narrative both the community of his day and the church of our day are authoritatively addressed by God. Now we are free to ask not whether, but in what way Luke's narrative might be normative for us in our reflection on the life of the church. We can allow his narrative to become for us, as it was for him, the vehicle of theology.

THE LITERARY DIFFICULTY

The basic shift comes in hearing Luke not first of all as a poor historian or even creative theologian whose perceptions may or may not be accurate, but as a prophetic witness, through whose words God's Word can be heard by believers. By being included in the canon, Luke's writing *as* writing has been certified by the community as a witness which speaks not only to its own time but to every time of the church, not only in its human voice, but in God's voice as well. I stress that it is not history which has been canonized and is therefore normative. *Compositions* are canonized and therefore stand as normative. It is not the reconstructed course of development in the early church which speaks to us, a reconstruction dependent on texts, but the writings given birth by the development which still speak today. Reading Luke-Acts in this way derives not from the decisions of scholarship, but from the decisions of faith within the church. When we allow the narrative itself to question us and our understanding, we listen to the voice of the New Testament writings as prophetic.

The shift, however, demands that we face another question. Is it genuinely the prophet's voice to which we attend, or only ours, projected onto the text? Even if we are not "doing history," isn't the "historical meaning" of the text necessary to maintain, if we are not to fly off into fancifulness? Yes, it is, but properly understood. The "historical meaning" of the text does not refer to the historical situation it addressed, but to the historical conditioning of the language of the text. Especially when these writings are read by a historical community which looks to them for its self-understanding, it is important that this literal, or historical, dimension of the text be the framework for the search. The historical dimension of the text is important precisely to maintain the "otherness" of the composition, preventing its precipitous appropriation by later readers. This conviction has long been held by Protestants, and was given magisterial expression for the Catholic Church in the Second Vatican Council's *Decree on Divine Revelation* 111, 12:

> However, since God speaks in sacred Scripture through men in human fashion, the interpreter of sacred Scripture, in order to see clearly what God wanted to communicate to us, should carefully investigate what meaning the sacred writers really intended, and what God wanted to manifest by means of their words.

Some literary critics are uncomfortable with the notion of "author's intention," thinking that it raises the impossible task of finding out what was in authors' heads when they wrote and limits the meaning of a text which, once released from the pen, begins a life of its own apart from the will of the writer. But so long as we do not confuse the philosophical notion of "intentionality" with psychological factors like "motivation" and "purpose," the concept of the author's intention is both necessary and helpful. After all, until a text *does* leave a writer's hand, it is in an organic and causal relationship with the writer in a way it is not to any subsequent reader. The text bears the marks of an author in a way different from the creative tracings of readers.

At any rate, the point of "intention" is not what was in the author's head, but what the author put on paper. If a text does not bear the impression of the author's thought and imagination, then it is not properly a "writing" at all. In poetry, worry about intentional fallacies may be in order. But it is over-fastidious in narratives, which at least purport to give accounts of real events. Structured narratives bear within themselves a certain "intentionality," whatever the state of mind of the ones who composed them. Finally, the point of respecting the author's intention, insofar as it is discernible in the text, is not to prohibit further meanings which new readers might discover, but to limit them to those which are consonant with the nature of the text. To ignore the historical linguistic conditioning of a text, therefore, is to subvert the text's ability to mediate a historical community's tradition.

If we are to discover Luke's intention, however, it can only be through the text itself. Even if we had some independent testimony from him as to what he wanted to say, it would not matter, unless he did in fact say it. Even then, Luke's view would be only another reader's opinion. To speak of the author's intention is in effect to look for the structure of the writing, its way of saying what it says. The meaning of a narrative, moreover, cannot be extracted from the text itself as a sort of residue. It inheres in the text as text. This means that not a summation or proposition, but the text itself must continually be read. The text shows its meaning fully as much in its "form" as in its "content." Indeed, the categories are hard to distinguish. This is true for all narratives, and is definitely the case in Luke-Acts, where the question about the author's intention must be answered in terms of the shape of the story the author tells.

The more Luke's method is uncovered by careful readers of his writing, the more convincing becomes the case that Luke intended his story as a whole to be the vehicle for his witness to the church. Study of the so-called summaries in Acts (e.g., 2:41-47; 4:32-37; 5:12-16) has shown that Luke tends to idealize, with an eye toward edification, situations historically more complex than his narrative would suggest. Analysis of the speeches in Acts (e.g., 2:14-36; 7:2-53; 13:16-41; 17:22-31) has led to a similar conclusion. Whatever traditional elements he uses in them, the perspective and placement of these speeches admirably serve Luke's narrative goals. The summaries and speeches serve a paradigmatic purpose.

What is true of these smaller units is also true of his story as a whole. The overall structure of Luke's story is critical to his purpose. Scholars have observed that Luke's careful formulation of the prologue to the Gospel expresses succinctly what he has actually accomplished in the writing. He tells his reader Theophilus that he wants to provide him with security or assurance concerning the things in which he had already been instructed (Luke 1:4). How will he accomplish this? By telling the story of how God has fulfilled his promises "in order" (*kathexes*; RSV "orderly account," Luke 1:3). "In order" is an especially revealing term. The sequence of the story is significant in Luke-Acts to a remarkable degree. How one thing follows after another seems almost as important as the things themselves. This is because the ordered form of memory itself has a convincing quality. If, therefore, the story of Luke-Acts is the means by which his literary and theological goals are met, then the story line is equally important for the appropriation of Luke-Acts by theological reflection. The story is the voice of this witness. The story the author tells is itself, as story, a datum of theology.

THE THEOLOGICAL DIFFICULTY

The force of the last proposition may become clearer when we seriously ask theological questions about the Apostolic Council as it is described in Acts 15. Wherein does it have significance for the church today, if it has any? Does its significance consist in the information it gives about church order (apostles and elders) in the early Christian community—if in fact Luke is accurately reporting and not reading them back from his own time? Perhaps a theologian could use this relatively less complex system as a reproach to a rigid hierarchical structure. That would be a helpful critical use. But the narrative is thereby reduced to supplying information, and information clearly of only secondary interest to the author himself. In this case, there would be no connection between theological appropriation and the literary shape of the text.

Is it, then, the actual decision of the Council which remains normative for the church today? If we take the wording of the decree literally, "that you abstain from what has been sacrificed to idols and from blood and from what is strangled and from unchastity" (Acts 15:29), that seems unlikely. The chastity part we might agree with, but few would want to argue that Christians should return to eating meat slaughtered only under kosher regulations. In fact, the textual variants of the decree testify to the checkered career it had in churches where Acts 15 was read. No, the content of the decree appears to stay fixed in the past, representing an important step in the development of the church, but no longer of critical relevance.

Perhaps the theological significance of the Council rests on the principles communicated by some of its participants, such as that spoken by Peter in 15:11: "We shall be saved through the grace of the Lord Jesus, just as they will." This is a statement of great importance. Taken with the still sharper sayings of Paul on the radical breakdown of human distinctions in Christ (e.g., 1 Cor. 7:17-24; 12:13; Gal. 3:27-29; Eph. 2:11-22; Col. 3:11), it stands as an enduring norm against which the church can measure itself. The principle, however, is found elsewhere, and, abstracted from the narrative, represents only a fraction of the passage's meaning.

What, then? I suggest that the prophetic witness of the Acts 15 *narrative* is critical to the theological reflection of the church because it gives the fullest picture in the New Testament of the *process* by which the church reaches decision. Only in Acts do we find a sustained treatment of the process by which the primitive church did or should have decided its future as God's people. Only here do we have so explicit a picture of the church as church articulating its faith in response to new and threatening circumstances. Furthermore, it is only in the narrative *as* narrative that this process is to be found. Acts 15 witnesses to the church concerning the way it reaches decisions, not by prescription, but by way of a paradigmatic story.

The church is not challenged by its hearing of this witness to imitate mechanically the steps taken by the characters in the story. The narrative, rather, invites us to consider the dynamics of decision making themselves, and to use this consideration when reflecting on the practice of the church wherever it exists. This narrative provides the theologian within the church with another and authoritative witness to the essential qualities necessary for the church to remain church as it decides hard questions.

A theological reading of Acts 15 would allow the biblical narrative to speak to the narratives of our own experience and self-understanding, that is, to pose the critical and interpretative questions to our own practices and presuppositions. The dynamics of the biblical story are to inform and, possibly, *reform* our own. The hearing of the biblical story, in short, should help us more keenly hear our own; the telling of the biblical story should give us the capacity to tell our own. We now turn to the hearing part of the task.

BIBLIOGRAPHICAL NOTE

For the sort of work done by New Testament scholars asking technical questions, one can begin with the commentary and helpful bibliography in Ernst Haenchen, *The Acts of the Apostles: A Commentary*, Eng. trans. B. Noble (Philadelphia: Westminster Press, 1971). The neglect of Acts 15 in the theology of the church can be seen, by way of example, in Hans Küng, *The Church* (New York: Doubleday & Co., 1976), and Jürgen Moltmann, *The Church in the Power of the Spirit* (New York: Harper & Row, 1978). Both writers also demonstrate the use of historical data to make theological judgments on Luke-Acts: so Küng, p. 238, and Moltmann, p. 298. Representative of scholarship on the church in the New Testament are the monographs by Eduard Schweizer, *Church Order in the New Testament*, Studies in Biblical Theology 32 (London: S.C.M. Press, 1961), and Rudolf Schnackenburg, *The Church in the New Testament*, Eng. trans. W. J. O'Hara (New York: Herder & Herder, 1965). The hopes and disappointments of "biblical theology" are well chronicled by Brevard Childs, *Biblical Theology in Crisis* (Philadelphia: Westminster Press, 1970). An instructive study of the neglect of narrative in the guild of biblical scholarship is Hans Frei's *The Eclipse of Biblical Narrative: A Study in Eighteenth and Nineteenth Century Hermeneutics* (New Haven: Yale University Press, 1974). For a stimulating discussion of the choices certain theologians have made regarding the authoritative use of Scripture, see David Kelsey, *The Uses of Scripture in Recent Theology* (Philadelphia: Fortress Press, 1975), and his more constructive theological proposal, "The Bible and Christian Theology," *The Journal of the American Academy of Religion* 48 (1980): 385-402. On the literary methods of Luke, see Luke T. Johnson, *The Literary Function of Possessions in Luke-Acts* (Missoula, Mont.: Scholars Press, 1977). A fuller bibliographical support for this chapter can be found in my unpublished paper submitted to the Luke-Acts Task Force of the Catholic Biblical Association in 1978, "The Use of Acts 15 in the Theology of the Church: A Scouting Report."

CHAPTER 5

DECISIONS

I have dealt only with the problems facing a theological interpretation of Acts 15. The same sort of considerations apply to the other narratives in Acts showing the church reaching decision (Acts 1:15-26; 4:23-31; 6:1-6; 9:26-30), which are less full and have received even less attention. In this chapter, I will first look at these shorter passages, since they precede Acts 15 and anticipate some of its important elements. When I return to Acts 15, I will consider it as part of a longer story, extending from the conversion of Cornelius to the end of the Apostolic Council (10:1–15:35). The cross-references in 15:7 and 15:24 to earlier events make this procedure necessary and useful. Acts 15 is the climax to a complex plot. Before looking at any of these narrative passages, however, it is helpful to place them within the outlook of Luke-Acts on decisions generally, for their very presence in a work so dominated by divine direction is somewhat startling.

DIVINE GUIDANCE AND HUMAN DECISIONS IN ACTS

Of all the characters who crowd the pages of Luke-Acts, God is the most active and dominant, directing the actions of the human figures. The prominence of God's guidance is not surprising, since Luke was trying to show how God fulfilled the promises through the things which had happened among his readers. The place for human freedom some-times seems small. Many of the stages of the gospel's progress to Rome, for example, take place under God's direct impulse. Thus, the angel of God releases Peter and John from prison to preach (5:19-21), and Peter from imprisonment a second time (12:6-17). The angel of the Lord and the Spirit guide Philip (8:26, 29, 39). The Holy Spirit selects Paul and Barnabas for mission in Antioch (13:1-3), forbids Paul's preaching in Asia (16:6-7), and drives Paul to his fateful journey to Jerusalem (20:22). Peter and John state the force of the divine direction succinctly when they declare that they cannot but proclaim (4:9), and must obey God rather than humans (5:29).

Other stages of the mission seem generated by circumstances arranged by God. Those scattered by persecution from Jerusalem preach in Samaria (8:4) and to the Hellenists in Antioch (11:19-21). In response, the Jerusalem leaders send Peter and John to confirm the Samaritan mission (8:14) and Barnabas the mission in Antioch (11:22). When Paul's preaching of Jesus as Messiah is rejected by Jews, he simply turns to the Gentiles, seeing in this the fulfillment of Scripture (see 13:46-47; 18:6; 28:25-28).

The narrative sometimes shows some interplay between human decision—or indecisiveness—and divine direction. Paul decided to go to Damascus to persecute "the Way" but is overturned and transformed (9:3ff.). Ananias's hesitancy to receive Paul is countered by a reassuring revelation (9:10-16). The decision of Paul to go to Macedonia is triggered by a vision (16:9-10). On the other side, Paul is told by the Spirit not to go to Jerusalem (21:4) and warned by prophecy what would face him there (21:11), but he still goes. Paul and Barnabas decide to part company on purely personal grounds, disagreeing over John-Mark (15:37-40). Finally, there is the short account of the disciples in Antioch collecting money for Jerusalem in response to prophecy (11:27-30).

With the partial exception of the last, these passages do not show us the church as *church* reaching decision. If we had only these texts we could learn that God intervenes in special ways to effect God's will, and that negative circumstances can turn out to be stages in the working out of God's plan. But we would learn nothing of how the human church might go about making decisions God had not already made for it.

FOUR CASES OF THE CHURCH MAKING DECISION

In contrast, there are four passages in Acts that show us the assembly acting as a group and reaching decision as a group. In each case the narrative discloses some aspects of the decision-making process.

The Election of Matthias (Acts 1:15-26)

In those days Peter stood up among the brethren (the company of persons was in all about a hundred and twenty), and said, "Brethren, the scripture had to be fulfilled, which the Holy Spirit spoke beforehand by the mouth of David, concerning Judas who was guide to those who arrested Jesus. For he was numbered among us, and was allotted his share in this ministry. (Now this man bought a field with the reward of his wickedness; and falling headlong he burst open in the middle and all his bowels gushed out. And it became known to all the inhabitants of Jerusalem, so that the field was called in their language Akeldama, that is, Field of Blood.) For it is written in the book of Psalms, 'Let his habitation become desolate / and let there be no one to live in it'; and 'His office let another take.' So one of the men who have accompanied us during all the time that the Lord Jesus went in and out among us, beginning from the baptism of John until the day when he was taken up from us—one of these men must become with us a witness to his resurrection." And they put forward two, Joseph called Barsabbas, who was surnamed Justus, and Matthias. And they prayed and said, "Lord, who knowest the hearts of all men, show which one of these two thou hast chosen to take the place in this ministry and apostleship from which Judas turned aside, to go to his own place." And they cast lots for them, and the lot fell on Matthias; and he was enrolled with the eleven apostles.

Jesus has ascended (Acts 1:6-11), having promised that the Holy Spirit would come on his followers (Luke 24:49; Acts 1:5). Those who came up from Galilee with Jesus were gathered in the upper room (Acts 1:13), where they "with one accord devoted themselves to prayer" (1:14), and waited for the Spirit. Before it comes, though, Luke shows us the assembly deliberating. Two issues need settling. Should Judas be replaced, and if so, by whom? The placement of this passage before Pentecost (2:1ff.) is important. By reaching this decision now, the community articulates its identity as Israel. The apostasy of Judas is significant because it broke the symbolic circle of the Twelve, who represent the restored Israel upon which the Spirit is to fall. That Judas' defection was seen as something more than a personal sin, indeed as a threat to the group, tells us something about the church's identity.

Peter's narrative dominates the passage. It is structured by the double "must" *(dei)* of 1:16 and 1:22. He first tells how the Scripture "had to be fulfilled." How? By telling the story of Judas' defection. Then he proposes the selection of a replacement, one who "must" become a witness of the resurrection. It is Peter's narrative which forms the basis for the proposal and the decision. The narrative does not baldly recite facts, but interprets the very psalm verses it invokes for authority. Peter cites verses of two psalms (Pss. 69:25, 109:8), which are found together only here in the New Testament. We see narrative and scriptural interpretation interpenetrate. Judas' apostasy is bracketed by "had to be fulfilled" and the citations themselves. The words of David from the past are now identified as "concerning Judas" in the present. Peter's rereading reveals implications of the text never anticipated by its original author. The decision to replace Judas is based on a theological interpretation of the event of his betrayal.

The prayer of the community contains another small, interpretative narrative (1:24-25). The strangest aspect of this passage occurs in the reference to the casting of lots: It makes clear that although the community nominates, it is God who discerns the hearts of all, who calls to apostleship. The assembly has been active throughout: It has listened to Peter's narrative and proposal; it has nominated two men (both steps involving discernment); it has prayed, cast lots, and enrolled Matthias among the other apostles, thus affirming as a community the decision revealed by God. As leader, Peter has narrated, interpreted the Scripture, and proposed action.

The Decision to Continue Preaching (Acts 4:23-31)

> When they were released they went to their friends and reported what the chief priests and the elders had said to them. And when they heard it, they lifted their voices together to God and said, "Sovereign Lord, who didst make the heaven and the earth and the sea and everything in them, who by the mouth of our father David, thy servant, didst say by the Holy Spirit, 'Why did the Gentiles rage, / and the peoples imagine vain things? / The kings of the earth set themselves in array, / and the rulers were gathered together, / against the Lord and against his Anointed'—for truly in this city there were gathered together against thy holy servant Jesus, whom thou didst anoint, both Herod and Pontius Pilate, with the Gentiles and the peoples of Israel, to do whatever thy hand and thy plan had predestined to take place. And now, Lord, look upon their threats, and grant to thy servants to speak thy word with all boldness, while thou stretchest out thy hand to heal, and signs and wonders are performed through the name of thy holy servant Jesus." And when they had prayed, the place in which they were gathered together was shaken; and they were all filled with the Holy Spirit and spoke the word of God with boldness.

It might be questioned whether this narrative deals with the church reaching decision, on two counts. First, although the RSV translates the Greek in 4:23 as "their friends" (*pros tous idious*), the phrase probably refers to the other apostles, rather than the whole assembly. Still, as we have seen already in the Matthias story, the apostles represent the church as a whole in this part of Acts. The second difficulty is whether a decision is really made. It is at best implicit, though its consequences are clear.

The passage is a watershed in this part of Acts. Before it, Peter and John are arrested and told to preach no more in Jesus' name (4:17). After it, the apostles preach with even greater power, working signs and wonders among the people and within the assembly (4:32–5:16), so that the Sanhedrin, for fear of being stoned, dare not stop them (5:17-42). The challenge posed for the group is that of persecution: Should they go on preaching in Jesus' name? Peter and John have already expressed their resolve (4:20), and now the group decides. It does so by the prayer for power in 4:24-30. The prayer is answered by an outpouring of the Spirit, which enables them to proclaim with still greater force (4:33).

The community prays in response to a narrative of fellow believers' experience. When they return to the group, Peter and John report on what happened to them. In the prayer, narrative and scriptural interpretation once more intermingle. The community cites Psalm 2:1-2, which speaks of kings and rulers gathered against the Lord's anointed. The psalmist had obviously written about opponents of a Davidic king. In the prayer, however, the community applies it to the opposition shown Jesus, "whom thou didst anoint" (Acts 4:27). This application of the Old Testament to the sufferings of the Messiah is not exceptional in the New Testament. Far more striking, though, is the way this interpretation is then applied directly to the situation of the community. As it is being persecuted, it remembers what Psalm 2 said about the sufferings of Jesus. This is not an automatic progression, but it is a remarkable one. The narrative of the community's experience extends the significance of the scriptural texts concerning the Messiah, so that they apply as well to the church of the Messiah. In the light of this, we are not surprised to find language otherwise applied to Jesus used in the prayer of the community for its own empowerment (4:29-30; cf. 2:22; 3:16). New experience leads to new understandings of texts, and therefore to a deeper self-understanding of the community itself. As in the election of Matthias, the community here listens to the narrative and prays. The leaders narrate and pray.

The Choosing of the Seven (Acts 6:1-6)

Now in these days when the disciples were increasing in number, the Hellenists murmured against the Hebrews because their widows were neglected in the daily distribution. And the twelve summoned the body of the disciples and said, "It is not right that we should give up preaching the word of God to serve tables. Therefore, brethren, pick out from among you seven men of good repute, full of the Spirit and of wisdom, whom we may appoint to this duty. But we will devote ourselves to prayer and to the ministry of the word." And what they said pleased the whole multitude, and they chose Stephen, a man full of faith and of the Holy Spirit, and Philip, and Prochorus, and Nicanor, and Timon, and Parmenas, and Nicolaus, a proselyte of Antioch. These they set before the apostles, and they prayed and laid their hands upon them.

This decision comes after the second unsuccessful attempt by the Sanhedrin to stop the apostles' preaching, and the grudging recognition by one of its members, "If it is of God, you will not be able to overthrow them" (5:39). The very success of the movement, however, created new difficulties. Like all Jewish communities, early Christian communities organized assistance for the needy, especially orphans and widows. On a daily basis, there was something like a soup kitchen. The growth of the church among both Aramaic-speaking and Greek-speaking synagogues within Jerusalem made this task complex and demanding. The ability of the apostles to continue overseeing the distribution of goods (cf. 4:35) was in doubt.

At an earlier stage, the distribution of possessions by the leaders served an important symbolic function for the community. It signified the reality and the style of apostolic authority (cf. 2:42-47; 4:32-37). The ministry of the word, indeed, was closely joined, already by Jesus, to table service (cf. Luke 9:10-17; 12:41-48; 22:24-30). The challenge facing the community, therefore, does not have to do simply with settling dissension. Nor does it concern the most efficient way to carry out a task, so that every constituency group's needs are met. It involves a deeper identity issue, and concerns the nature of spiritual authority, its symbolization, and its transmission.

The multiplicity of factors at work in this passage makes it difficult to read at the level of historical inquiry. Ostensibly, the community decides who will care for widows among the Greek-speaking believers in Jerusalem. But in fact, the men appointed for the task never perform it. Instead, just like the Twelve, they go about preaching and performing wonders, only within a different constituency (cf. Acts 6:8; 8:5). The apparent inconsistency can best be accounted for by recognizing the symbolic nature of the decision. Appointing seven servants of the table for a different segment of the population symbolizes the transmission of spiritual authority to these men for another part of God's people, authority to preach and work wonders in the name of Jesus. In turn, the decision made by the church rendered more explicit its understanding of the apostolic office. It may have been symbolized by table fellowship, but its essence was preaching (6:2), prayer, and the ministry of the word (6:4).

The process of reaching decision here bears some resemblance to the two previous passages: The assembly as a whole is gathered by the Twelve (6:2), and there is a formal prayer by all before the laying on of hands (6:6). There is no narrative of experience here, only the simple statement of their proposal by the Twelve, which responds to what the author clearly intends for us to understand as the community's shared narrative—that is, its increasingly chronic experience of conflict and need. Nor is there any invocation of Scripture to interpret the situation. In this case, the role of the assembly is more active. They discern the words of the Twelve, and are "pleased": That is, they give consent (6:5). The assembly chooses (literally, "elects") those whom it recognizes as "full of the Spirit and of wisdom" (6:3) to be ministers, another act of discernment. These candidates they place before the Twelve. The Greek text does not make clear whether the whole assembly or only the Twelve lay hands on the seven, and the evidence from elsewhere in Acts is too mixed for certainty either way (cf. 8:17-18; 9:17; 13:3; 19:6). At the least, the community listens, approves, chooses, and prays. The leaders state, propose, pray, and ordain.

The Acceptance of Paul as a Disciple (9:26-30)

> And when he had come to Jerusalem he attempted to join the disciples; and they were all afraid of him, for they did not believe that he was a disciple. But Barnabas took him, and brought him to the apostles, and declared to them how on the road he had seen the Lord, who spoke to him, and how at Damascus he had preached boldly in the name of Jesus. So he went in and out among them at Jerusalem, preaching boldly in the name of the Lord. And he spoke and disputed against the Hellenists; but they were seeking to kill him. And when the brethren knew it, they brought him down to Caesarea, and sent him off to Tarsus.

This brief account takes place after Paul's conversion (9:1-19) and after a short but stormy sojourn in Damascus (9:20-25). He returns to Jerusalem, not as a persecutor of "the Way," but as one who wishes to "join the disciples" (9:26). This is obviously a threatening circumstance for the community. How can it trust one who was only a short time before seeking to eradicate it? Was Paul's request simply a ruse to gain the names of others he could arrest? The real issue would seem to be whether or not to flee this man's presence, not whether to accept him as a fellow disciple. But that is what Paul wants, and his desire must be considered. Naturally enough, the group's instinct for self-preservation dominates at first: "They were all afraid of him, for they did not believe that he was a disciple" (9:26). Barnabas now reenters the narrative of Acts. We saw him first as one who donated his possessions to the community and who received a new name from the apostles (4:36-37). He is a trusted member of the community. He takes Paul to the leaders and "narrates to them" (RSV "declared to them," 9:27) Paul's experiences: his vision, his dialogue with the risen Lord, his preaching in Damascus (9:27). The decision made by the disciples is not explicitly stated, but it is clear from the sequel: Paul moves about freely, preaching in the name of Jesus (9:28). And when he meets opposition and the danger of death, the church rallies to help him and sends him safely to Tarsus (9:29-30).

The church's decision is, on the face of it, remarkable enough: To accept as a fellow believer one who, only a short time before, was actively persecuting the group is bold discernment, indeed. But even more stunning is the basis for the decision. It is not *Paul's* own narration, but Barnabas' recital of Paul's story that convinces the apostles. For Barnabas to do this, he first had to hear Paul's story and believe it. When he relates the events to the apostles, he does so not as a neutral reporter, but as one who has adopted Paul's own viewpoint: On the way, Paul saw the Lord (9:27). This narrative, we understand, had convincing power. It enabled the community to accept Paul as a fellow believer, because in the narrative they could discern the work of the Lord. There is no citation of Scripture here; only the narrative of experience. And it is a narrative mediated to the community for an outsider by a trusted member of the church. We see the possibility of a narrative being heard from the outside because it is taken up by members of the community and made their own.

In these four passages, we have seen the church as church reaching decision. No set literary "form" characterizes all these accounts, but there is some consistency. One or another element may be missing, and what is central to one account may be peripheral to another. But we find in them the open interaction of the assembly and its leaders through public speech. We see a role for prayer by the assembly; for the narrative of experience; for interpreting Scripture in the light of that experience. In each passage, we also find situations, which could have been understood in a purely negative fashion (the apostasy of an apostle, persecution, dissension, the approach of a foe) turned, by means of narrative and interpretation, into the basis for positive community decision.

The correctness of the decisions is not always immediately clear. At the election of Matthias, the lots show divine approval; at the prayer for power, the Spirit makes its presence felt. But for the choosing of the seven, only subsequent experience validates the decision: When all but the apostles are scattered, these new ministers carry the message afield. In the case of Paul, the results remain ambiguous. His acceptance by the church immediately brings trouble upon it, and Paul stays on rather uneasy terms with the Jerusalem church (cf. 15:1ff.; 21:18-25).

These passages are not much more than thumbnail sketches. We can guess at the complexity of human motivation and circumstance beneath the surface. But the text shows nothing of the indecision, hesitancy, and conflict we suspect is always present when people try to make sense of their experience in the church. These decisions still bear the marks of inevitability. Only when we read the complete story of the conversion of Cornelius and the Jerusalem Council do we find a fully nuanced picture of the church reaching decision, where human frailty and the divine will are both impressively displayed.

FROM CORNELIUS TO COUNCIL: STAGES OF A CHURCH DECISION

The conversion of Cornelius created a crisis because he was a Gentile. Peter's baptism of Cornelius and his household (Acts 10:48) anticipated a far more extensive mission to the Gentile world (14:27). Since before that conversion, the church, according to Luke, had been only Jewish, the innovation demanded a discernment both of the church and of this challenge. Was the conversion of the Gentiles legitimate? If so, on what grounds could they be considered part of God's people? It is not necessary to ask whether Cornelius was, historically, the first Gentile convert, or whether Peter really anticipated Paul (or the Hellenistic missionaries) in taking this critical initiative. The point is that Luke shows us the process by which the church decided the issue, how it reached its decision.

The importance of the decision is shown by the placement of the account and the close attention it receives. Chapter 15 is the principal turning point in the book of Acts. Before it, the Jerusalem mission dominates; after it, attention is almost exclusively focused on Paul's preaching all the way to Rome. The significance of the turning point can be grasped, however, only when Acts 15 is recognized as the climax to a story beginning in Acts 10. Nowhere else in Luke's writing do we find such painstaking attention to minute detail at each stage of the action. His narrative elsewhere moves lightly and rapidly. Here, it pauses, recapitulates, and reinterprets itself. The author does not want the reader to miss the meaning of these events.

The narrative attention to human doubt and debate is all the more impressive, since Luke has shown the reader from the beginning of his composition that God intended the salvation of the Gentiles. The salvation brought by Jesus to Israel is a "light of revelation to the Gentiles" (Luke 2:32), and when John the Baptist precedes him in preaching, the Isaiah passage in Luke's version includes the words, "All flesh shall see the salvation of God" (Luke 3:6; cf. Isa. 40:5, LXX). The sending out of the seventy-(two) by Jesus in Luke 10:1-12 is often regarded as an anticipation of the Gentile mission, and may well be. After his resurrection, Jesus tells his witnesses that "forgiveness of sins should be preached in his name to all nations, beginning from Jerusalem" (Luke 24:47), and just before his ascension, he tells the eleven they will be his witnesses "to the end of the earth" (Acts 1:8). At Pentecost, Peter proclaims that the promise of the Holy Spirit is for those Jews who hear him and for "all that are far off, every one whom the Lord our God calls to him" (Acts 2:39). In a later speech, he declares that to the Jerusalemite Jews has Jesus been sent "first," suggesting that if they receive the prophet, the promise to Abraham will be fulfilled, for "in your posterity shall all the families of the earth be blessed" (Acts 3:25-26; see Gen. 22:18). We have also seen how the Holy Spirit directed the preaching to the Samaritans and the Ethiopian eunuch (Acts 8:4-40), though Luke may have regarded them as part of the restoration of Israel. In short, Luke has left his reader in no doubt concerning God's intention: From the beginning, God has willed the salvation of the Gentile world.

The standpoint of the storyteller, which is shared with the reader, makes the event appear inevitable. It is the more striking, then, that Luke is so concerned to show the *human process* of coming to recognize and affirm God's intention. To find the dynamics of decision making in this story, we must follow the plot sequentially. The process and the issues emerge slowly and in definite progression. Whether Gentiles can be preached to or even baptized is settled rather quickly. But the deeper human difficulty of fellowship between Jewish and Gentile believers is far harder to resolve. If both Jews and Gentiles are to be considered part of "God's people," will it be on even or uneven footing? On what basis will Gentiles be recognized and associated with? On the basis of their belief in the Messiah and the gift of the Holy Spirit, or on the basis of being circumcised and observing the law of Moses? Will the church split into two ethnically and ritually distinct bodies? Is Yahweh a tribal deity, or Lord of all? Will fellowship be determined by faith, or by precedent;

by the experience of God, or by the rules of the community? At stake is the church's identity as witness to the work of God. Will the church decide to recognize and acknowledge actions of God that go beyond its present understanding, or will it demand that God work within its categories?

The First Decision: The Conversion (Acts 10:1-48)

At Caesarea there was a man named Cornelius, a centurion of what was known as the Italian Cohort, a devout man who feared God with all his household, gave alms liberally to the people, and prayed constantly to God. About the ninth hour of the day he saw clearly in a vision an angel of God coming in and saying to him, "Cornelius." And he stared at him in terror, and said, "What is it, Lord?" And he said to him, "Your prayers and your alms have ascended as a memorial before God. And now send men to Joppa, and bring one Simon who is called Peter; he is lodging with Simon, a tanner, whose house is by the seaside." When the angel who spoke to him had departed, he called two of his servants and a devout soldier from among those that waited on him, and having related everything to them, he sent them to Joppa.

The next day, as they were on their journey and coming near the city, Peter went up on the housetop to pray, about the sixth hour. And he became hungry and desired something to eat; but while they were preparing it, he fell into a trance and saw the heaven opened, and something descending, like a great sheet, let down by four corners upon the earth. In it were all kinds of animals and reptiles and birds of the air. And there came a voice to him, "Rise, Peter; kill and eat." But Peter said, "No, Lord; for I have never eaten anything that is common or unclean." And the voice came to him again a second time, "What God has cleansed, you must not call common." This happened three times, and the thing was taken up at once to heaven.

Now while Peter was inwardly perplexed as to what the vision which he had seen might mean, behold, the men that were sent by Cornelius, having made inquiry for Simon's house, stood before the gate and called out to ask whether Simon who was called Peter was lodging there. And while Peter was pondering the vision, the Spirit said to him, "Behold, three men are looking for you. Rise and go down, and accompany them without hesitation; for I have sent them." And Peter went down to the men and said, "I am the one you are looking for; what is the reason for your coming?" And they said, "Cornelius, a centurion, an upright and God-fearing man, who is well spoken of by the whole Jewish nation, was directed by a holy angel to send for you to come to his house, and to hear what you have to say." So he called them in to be his guests.

The story begins, we notice, with the religious experience of someone outside the historical people of God. God begins this work with the Gentile, Cornelius. Although he is not circumcised and a member of

God's people, he is nevertheless one who fears God and prays intensely (10:2). It is in prayer that he has the vision which begins this critical series of events. The vision of God's angel, whom Cornelius calls "Lord," is exceedingly short and to the point: "Send . . . and bring one Simon who is called Peter." Cornelius obeys the order without question or hesitation. He "narrates" all (RSV "related everything," 10:8) to his delegates, so they can adequately inform Peter. The intrusion of the Holy (see the "terror" of Cornelius in 10:4) and the divine direction are explicit here, but they require human trust and obedience to become effective.

Luke then shows us Simon Peter having a vision as well, while the men from Cornelius are on the road. He, too, is at prayer (10:9-16), but in contrast to Cornelius' experience, Peter's vision is complex and confusing. He rejects the order to eat clean and unclean food indiscriminately, on the basis of his previous experience and religious self-understanding as a pious Jew (10:14). He is not so quick as the Gentile Cornelius to heed the voice, even though the vision and its gnomic command, "What God has cleansed, you must not call common," is repeated three times (10:15-16). Peter not only refuses the order but is thrown into utter confusion by his experience. Was it only a projection of his desires, since he was at the time so hungry (10:10)? Luke tells us that Peter was "inwardly perplexed as to what the vision which he had seen might mean" (10:17). This confusion is emphasized in Acts 10:19. While Peter continues "pondering the vision," the men arrive from Cornelius (10:17). The Spirit now gives Peter a definite nudge, telling him to go with them "without hesitation." The Greek of this phrase can also be translated "without discrimination" (10:20), and both senses are appropriate here. Peter listens to the men "narrate" what they had been told by Cornelius. We notice that the message in their retelling is now slightly elaborated, including the purpose clause "to hear what you have to say" in 10:22. The narrative of Cornelius' experience as relayed by these men provides Peter with the first interpretation of his vision, and the basis for his first decision: "So he called them in to be his guests" (10:23). The "so" in this sentence is very definite in the Greek, indicating that Peter's response was to what he had heard from the men.

The importance of Peter's first response should be clear. Even though not fully understanding the direction of God given by the coincidence of vision and visit, he obeys it. Peter receives Gentiles into his abode as guests. He makes, in this gesture, no discrimination. In this first scene, we see that the separate religious experience of two persons—one inside the church, one outside it—is mediated by narrative to form the basis for a common story. By believing the testimony of the messengers, Peter allows his own ambiguous experience to be interpreted. He is an individual believer discerning and deciding on behalf of God within the complexity and confusion of real life.

> The next day he rose and went off with them, and some of the brethren from Joppa accompanied him. And on the following day they entered Caesarea. Cornelius was expecting them and had called together his kinsmen and close friends. When Peter entered, Cornelius met him and fell down at his feet and worshiped him. But Peter lifted him up, saying, "Stand up; I too am a man." And as he talked with him, he went in and found many persons gathered; and he said to them, "You yourselves know how unlawful it is for a Jew to associate with or to visit any one of another nation; but God has shown me that I should not call any man common or unclean. So when I was sent for, I came without objection. I ask then why you sent for me."
>
> And Cornelius said, "Four days ago, about this hour, I was keeping the ninth hour of prayer in my house; and behold, a man stood before me in bright apparel, saying, 'Cornelius, your prayer has been heard and your alms have been remembered before God. Send therefore to Joppa and ask for Simon who is called Peter; he is lodging in the house of Simon, a tanner, by the seaside.' So I sent to you at once, and you have been kind enough to come. Now therefore we are all here present in the sight of God, to hear all that you have been commanded by the Lord."
>
> And Peter opened his mouth and said: "Truly I perceive that God shows no partiality, but in every nation any one who fears him and does what is right is acceptable to him."

The fact that some of Peter's Jewish Christian associates accompany him from Joppa to Caesarea (10:23) is of considerable importance for the rest of the story. They are also believers ("brethren"), and their presence raises Peter's act from the private to the communal level. They will witness the events still to follow. In the meantime, Cornelius also gathers associates (10:24). Something more than a private encounter is about to take place. Peter has stopped questioning by Acts 10:27-28. He speaks with Cornelius and goes in with him to the larger gathering, another critical step for Peter. He has begun to see the implications of his vision, and he acts on them. He gives voice to his understanding in 10:28: "God has shown me that I should not call any man common or unclean." This is *not*, of course, literally what the voice from the vision had said. Only Peter's subsequent experience, shaped by Cornelius' narrative, has led him to this interpretation of the vision. He now understands the beasts as standing for peoples. The full meaning of "what God has cleansed" is still not clear to him. So Peter asks Cornelius to tell him more (10:29)!

Cornelius tells again, firsthand, the narrative of his religious experience (10:30-33). It contains still another interpretative addition concerning Peter's coming. Now he says that everyone is gathered in God's presence "to hear all that you have been commanded by the Lord" (10:33), a refinement of "to hear what you have to say" added by the men in 10:22. As a result of his meeting and conversation with Peter (10:27), Cornelius' expectation grows, as well as his own awareness of what his vision meant.

Peter responds to the narrative by stating in solemn fashion his own conclusion. He has now come to see what God had been trying to tell him all along. In Cornelius' story, mention was made of prayer and almsgiving, and Peter picks this up in his own statement: "In every nation any one who fears him and does what is right is acceptable to him" (10:35). The RSV translation, "doing right," misses the allusion built into the Greek, "does justice." "Doing justice" is, in this tradition, equivalent to almsgiving, a work of mercy. And prayer is the acting out of "fear of God" (cf. 10:2). Peter's insight has radical significance. God has led him to see that it is not membership in a certain people which makes one acceptable to God, but the human response of "faith"—another way of saying "fear of God"—which is spelled out in mercy. And this is found among all peoples.

Peter also sees that this acceptance by God is not accidental or arbitrary, but is rooted in God's nature. There is "no respecting of persons" with God. In the language of this tradition, the phrase refers to the sort of prejudice or partiality judges might show when given bribes (see Lev. 19:15). God is not that sort of judge. God's righteousness is not swayed by considerations of ethnic origin or religious affiliation. Peter now realizes that God is God of the Gentiles as well as of the Jews. The God worshiped in the church is not a tribal deity (cf. also Rom. 2:11; 3:29-30). Peter also sees the implications. If the Gentiles are acceptable to *God*, then they ought also to be acceptable to the *church*, which claims to witness to God. On this basis, then, he makes the decision to preach the gospel to Cornelius and his household.

> "You know the word which he sent to Israel, preaching good news of peace by Jesus Christ (he is Lord of all), the word which was proclaimed throughout all Judea, beginning from Galilee after the baptism which John preached: how God anointed Jesus of Nazareth with the Holy Spirit and with power; how he went about doing good and healing all that were oppressed by the devil, for God was with him. And we are witnesses to all that he did both in the country of the Jews and in Jerusalem. They put him to death by hanging him on a tree; but God raised him on the third day and made him manifest; not to all the people but to us who were chosen by God as witnesses, who ate and drank with him after he rose

from the dead. And he commanded us to preach to the people, and to testify that he is the one ordained by God to be judge of the living and the dead. To him all the prophets bear witness that every one who believes in him receives forgiveness of sins through his name."

While Peter was still saying this, the Holy Spirit fell on all who heard the word. And the believers from among the circumcised who came with Peter were amazed, because the gift of the Holy Spirit had been poured out even on the Gentiles. For they heard them speaking in tongues and extolling God. Then Peter declared, "Can any one forbid water for baptizing these people who have received the Holy Spirit just as we have?" And he commanded them to be baptized in the name of Jesus Christ. Then they asked him to remain for some days.

Peter's message for the household of Cornelius is itself a narrative of the events to which he and his fellows are witnesses (10:39, 41). Peter's story begins where the gospel does, with the "word which [God] sent to Israel" through Jesus' preaching of peace (10:36), and ends with the realization he had just had in a deeper fashion than before, "every one who believes in him receives forgiveness of sins through his name" (10:43). Is it by accident that, in this context, Peter stresses that part of the narrative that concerns the table fellowship between the risen Lord and his followers? It is clearly what is most pertinent to the challenge now being posed to the church, concerning how that circle of table fellowship can be enlarged. Remembering the story enables it to move forward. The statement that this gift is available to his Gentile listeners precipitates a new religious experience among them. While they are still listening, the Holy Spirit falls on them (10:44).

The reaction of the onlookers is especially interesting. We remember that they are Jewish believers who had accompanied Peter from Joppa (10:23). They are more than passive witnesses. They are the ones who identify the event's meaning. They hear people speaking in tongues and praising God, and conclude on that basis that the Holy Spirit has been given to the Gentiles as well (Acts 10:45-46). From the effect, they deduce the cause. How could they exercise this discernment? Because they themselves had first experienced the Spirit in such a fashion. Because they know from their own story that the Holy Spirit gifted them with ecstasy and praise (Acts 2:1-4), they can recognize the same gift here. Peter's question to them presupposes such a shared recognition. The Gentiles have received the Holy Spirit "just as we have" (10:47). No words of the prophets or of the Law are used to interpret this event, but the previous religious experience of the witnesses is used to provide a preliminary validation. This enables them to discern the movement of God's Spirit in the present. On the basis of this recognition, Peter orders

the people to be baptized (10:48). He has come to a still deeper understanding of his initial vision. Those he had previously thought unclean
have been gifted by God's Spirit in the same way he had. This awareness
has resulted from his own experience, the narrative of others' experience, and his witnessing the religious experience of others. From this, he
has come to recognize God at work, and has the Gentiles baptized.
Peter's decision is for God. The ritual acceptance into the church follows
the perception that God has already accepted them into his people.

The Decision Defended: Peter in Jerusalem (Acts 11:1-18)

Now the apostles and the brethren who were in Judea heard that the
Gentiles also had received the word of God. So when Peter went up to
Jerusalem, the circumcision party criticized him, saying, "Why did you go
to uncircumcised men and eat with them?" But Peter began and explained
to them in order: "I was in the city of Joppa praying; and in a trance I saw
a vision, something descending, like a great sheet, let down from heaven
by four corners; and it came down to me. Looking at it closely I observed
animals and beasts of prey and reptiles and birds of the air. And I heard
a voice saying to me, 'Rise, Peter; kill and eat.' But I said, 'No, Lord; for
nothing common or unclean has ever entered my mouth.' But the voice
answered a second time from heaven, 'What God has cleansed you must
not call common.' This happened three times, and all was drawn up again
into heaven. At that very moment three men arrived at the house in which
we were, sent to me from Caesarea. And the Spirit told me to go with them,
making no distinction. These six brethren also accompanied me, and we
entered the man's house. And he told us how he had seen the angel
standing in his house and saying, 'Send to Joppa and bring Simon called
Peter; he will declare to you a message by which you will be saved, you
and all your household.' As I began to speak, the Holy Spirit fell on them
just as on us at the beginning. And I remembered the word of the Lord,
how he said, 'John baptized with water, but you shall be baptized with the
Holy Spirit.' If then God gave the same gift to them as he gave to us when
we believed in the Lord Jesus Christ, who was I that I could withstand
God?" When they heard this they were silenced. And they glorified God,
saying, "Then to the Gentiles also God has granted repentance unto life."

This is an altogether astonishing passage. Precisely its apparent re-
dundancy within the larger plot forces us to recognize the significance
of the previous event and the need for it to be ratified. Here we see Peter's
individual decision challenged by certain members of his home community (11:3), and then affirmed by the community as a whole (11:18). We
learn from this that opposition, openly expressed, is part of the decision-
making process. It enables discernment to take place, by exposing the
options to full view. It is part of the testing of the Spirit. When the church

argues over its actions, it discovers the roots of its implicit understanding which gave rise to the action, and it can begin to articulate its faith in a more explicit way.

We see that the issue of relations with Gentiles in the church is now reaching the level of church discussion and discernment, properly speaking. It is natural in this case that those from "the circumcision party" should criticize Peter (11:2). Their attack, however, is not directed to his baptizing the Gentiles, but returns to the stage of Peter's first understanding. They attack his having eaten with Gentiles (11:3), that is, having fellowship with them. The issue of communion is explicitly raised. Just because Gentiles have "received the word of God" (which is acknowledged in 11:1), it does not necessarily follow that they should have full communion with Jewish believers, or be considered as members of God's people in the fullest sense.

The problem is a real one. For a Jew to eat without attending to ritual purity meant to lose his or her Jewish identity. Part of ritual purity, however, means to not "give dogs what is holy" (Matt. 7:6). How can meals be sacred, yet shared with unclean people? His opponents imply that Peter has, by eating with Gentiles, himself gone against his identity as one of God's people, and has, furthermore, jeopardized the identity of the community.

To answer the challenge, Peter is required to show the deeper implications of the Gentiles' conversion. The Gentile believers, he says, received the same gift as did the Jewish believers in the beginning (11:15). Thus we see the narrative pertinence of Peter's taking along his Jewish associates. Peter stresses that he took along "these six brethren" and that "we" entered the house (11:12). Something more than a clever rhetorical ploy comes into play here. Peter is calling his associates to witness—as Jews—to the accuracy of his narrative. More than that, they must now stand on *their* own experience, for they were involved from the start, and had been, in fact, the ones who had certified that the Gentiles were receiving the Holy Spirit. If these six brethren now dispute Peter's account on other grounds, they run the risk of denying their own experience of God's power.

Of greater importance for our investigation of the decision-making process is the *manner* in which Peter responds. When challenged, he does not stand on his authority as an apostle, or argue from the Scripture, for neither really covers the situation. He neither argues nor asserts. Rather, he *narrates* his own experience. This and this alone moves the others to accept and ratify his decision. Peter tells them, in effect, that from the first vision on, he was led to understand that God was at work in these events. Thus we feel the force of his final question, framed as a simple conditional, "If then God gave the same gift to them . . . who was I that I could withstand God?" (11:17). Peter states it neatly. To refuse to recognize the clear evidence of God's action is to oppose God.

Two further aspects of the passage deserve some attention. First, Peter narrates these events "in order" (11:4). This is the same term used by Luke in the prologue to the Gospel (Luke 1:3), and has considerable significance. By telling the gospel story "in order," Luke wishes to give his reader "security" or "certainty." So here, by telling his tale "in order," Peter's narrative, we understand, has a convincing quality. The narrative itself is the vehicle of persuasion.

The second aspect of Peter's story is even more intriguing. We find two important additions to the story this time around. In 11:14, Cornelius' vision is given its final elaboration: He can expect from Peter a message "by which you will be saved." The past is shaped by the realization granted by the present. Another and even more exciting addition is found in 11:16, where Peter says he remembered the word of the Lord when he saw the Holy Spirit fall on the Gentiles. The experience of the present selects what is remembered from the past. This outpouring of the Spirit stimulates Peter's recall of Jesus' words on the Spirit. In Luke-Acts, however, the saying he remembers is not one of the earthly but of the resurrected Lord. He told it to those waiting for the baptism of the Holy Spirit at Pentecost (Acts 1:5). That was, however, a small band of Jewish disciples. When Peter sees these Gentiles receive the Holy Spirit, he remembers Jesus' words, but with an entirely new application. What Jesus said to Jews is seen to apply to Gentiles as well. The words of Jesus are given new import because of the continuing work of the Spirit. The experience of God's activity in the present acts as a key for the interpretation of the Scripture, and now, we see, for the sayings of Jesus as well.

The Jerusalem community recognizes that the Gentiles have "been given the gift of repentance unto life," but the issue of relations has not been solved. The implications of God's will and Peter's decision have not yet been articulated by the church as a whole. The question whether Gentiles must become Jewish before they can be part of the people of God still remains. And if they do not, how can Jewish believers associate with them, and still be faithful to their understanding of God's revelation?

The Decision Opposed and Affirmed:
The Jerusalem Council (Acts 14:26–15:35)

After the confrontation between Peter and the Judean brethren, and before the Apostolic Council, Luke shows how the preaching to the

Gentiles became more than a singular and private decision. He tells how "Greeks" were evangelized in Antioch (11:19-26), and how the missionary journey of Paul and Barnabas became, in Antioch of Pisidia, a mission to the Gentiles as well (13:46-48). In contrast to the Cornelius episode, these steps are not accompanied by agonizing deliberation, but appear to be directed by God through circumstances. The work is certified in the first instance by the sending of Barnabas to Antioch from Jerusalem (11:22), and in the second by the signs and wonders God worked through Paul and Barnabas among the Gentiles (15:12). The Gentiles are becoming Christians now in many places. More than a purely local decision, therefore, is required on the issues already raised concerning conversion and communion. The narrative shows us next how these questions build to conscious church decision, and shows us how the process of reaching decision is a theological process.

> And from there they sailed to Antioch, where they had been commended to the grace of God for the work which they had fulfilled. And when they arrived, they gathered the church together and declared all that God had done with them, and how he had opened a door of faith to the Gentiles. And they remained no little time with the disciples.
> But some men came down from Judea and were teaching the brethren, "Unless you are circumcised according to the custom of Moses, you cannot be saved." And when Paul and Barnabas had no small dissension and debate with them, Paul and Barnabas and some of the others were appointed to go up to Jerusalem to the apostles and the elders about this question. So, being sent on their way by the church, they passed through both Phoenicia and Samaria, reporting the conversion of the Gentiles, and they gave great joy to all the brethren.

A conflict that originates in the Church of Antioch makes the Jerusalem Council necessary. The Antioch controversy is generated by the return of Paul and Barnabas from their first missionary trip. They gather the church and narrate what God has done through them, how God has "opened a door of faith to the Gentiles" (14:27; cf. 13:48). The Church of Antioch is next visited by another party, "some men from Judea" (15:1). We remember that Paul and Barnabas belong to this Antiochian community; they were sent out by it (13:1-3) and have fulfilled its mission (14:26). These other men are interlopers. And that makes their charge all the more insidious. They say, "You cannot be saved . . ." (15:1). They are saying this to the brothers, that is, the believers at Antioch. They are challenging not only the mission of Paul and Barnabas, but the integrity of the Antiochian Church itself, which, it appears, consisted at least in part of Gentiles (cf. 11:20). We remember now that this church had already been approved by Jerusalem when Barnabas had confirmed the work of God there (11:22). By challenging the Antioch community at the level of its own salvation, the Judeans put the question in its starkest terms: Is the grace of God and the gift of the Holy Spirit sufficient for salvation, or not? And this touches another question: Is God's work going to be acknowledged as it manifests itself, or only as it conforms to the church's presuppositions?

The narrative shows no embarrassment at this opposition or the intensity of the debate it generates. There was "no small dissension and debate" (15:2). Luke uses phrases like these for emphasis (cf. 14:28); we are to infer a great turmoil. Here, as with Peter before the Judean brethren (11:3), open opposition is part of the discernment process. The assembly in Antioch is active throughout. They are gathered to hear the narrative of Paul and Barnabas, and after the dispute "they" send representatives to Jerusalem (15:2). The Greek does not make it clear whom they send. The "some of the others" could refer to the opponents of Paul and Barnabas. In this case, the church would have sent as a delegation both parties to the dispute. It is more likely, however, that those who were sent off share the views of Barnabas and Paul, for as they travel they "narrate" to other churches "the conversion of the Gentiles" and stir up enthusiasm for this initiative (15:3). The sending of a delegation from Antioch indicates the willingness of the daughter church to hear the judgment of the apostles and elders in Jerusalem on this issue (15:2). At the same time, it is something of a confrontation. Jerusalem had once approved this community, but now those who came from Judea were disturbing it. Was Jerusalem going back on its word and breaking fellowship? The representatives from Antioch have witnessed God at work among them, and in the mission carried out by Paul and Barnabas. This difficulty was created not by internal dissension, but by attack from the outside. The Antiochian group is therefore going to the source of the trouble, to call the Jerusalem Church to account. This is a matter, after all, which affects the integrity of the Antiochian Church's existence as "Christian."

So casual is the mention of Paul and Barnabas narrating their experiences to the churches in Phoenicia and Samaria that one can almost miss it and its significance. It shows us again the power of narrative to convince. But it also shows us how the issue raised in Antioch is of concern to other communities. This is no longer just a local dispute, but a challenge which must be decided by the church as such.

> When they came to Jerusalem, they were welcomed by the church and the apostles and the elders, and they declared all that God had done with them. But some believers who belonged to the party of the Pharisees rose

up, and said, "It is necessary to circumcise them, and to charge them to keep the law of Moses."

The whole Church of Jerusalem, with its leaders, greets the delegation from Antioch. The assembly as such is given the chance to hear both sides of the debate, for the ultimate discernment and decision rests with it. The conflict is stated sharply. The party from Antioch narrates once more "all that God had done with them." Their position is communicated best by recounting their experience of God's work. Notice that this includes not only what God had done through Paul and Barnabas in the mission field, but also what God had done "with them."

The Pharisaic party, on the other hand, argues on the basis of theological principle and precedent. Their "it is necessary," we assume, rests on those warrants. Because of the way this story finally ends, it is easy to dismiss these "legalists" and their position. For us to appreciate the decision that was made, however, it is important to recognize the force of their position. It was theologically respectable. If part of God's revelation consisted in the practice of circumcision as the symbol of entrance into the people (and it did); and if all the previous revelation by God had taught the necessity of keeping the Law as a full part of being the people and receiving its blessing (as it surely did); then their statement is neither superficial nor silly. In fact, the weight of the evidence would seem to be on their side.

The only thing which could counter such a powerful precedent is the conviction that the God revealed in the past was active in these events now, and that God's way of maintaining continuity in revelation may not be the same as ours. This, then, becomes the issue for the church's discernment. Will it fall back on its deeply rooted (and revealed) perceptions of how God "ought" to act, or will it recognize that God moves ahead of its perceptions? Perhaps an anticipation of the outcome can be seen in the very reception of the delegation from Antioch. Like Peter with Cornelius, the act of hospitality is already a kind of recognition.

The apostles and the elders were gathered together to consider this matter. And after there had been much debate, Peter rose and said to them, "Brethren, you know that in the early days God made choice among you, that by my mouth the Gentiles should hear the word of the gospel and believe. And God who knows the heart bore witness to them, giving them the Holy Spirit just as he did to us; and he made no distinction between us and them, but cleansed their hearts by faith. Now therefore why do you make trial of God by putting a yoke upon the neck of the disciples which neither our fathers nor we have been able to bear? But we believe that we shall be saved through the grace of the Lord Jesus, just as they will."

> And all the assembly kept silence; and they listened to Barnabas and Paul as they related what signs and wonders God had done through them among the Gentiles.

After the public statement of positions, it appears that the matter is left for the debate of the apostles and elders who gather together (15:6). The larger assembly is still present and the discussion takes place before them (see 15:12, 22), but the leaders now actively articulate the question. After that initial sharp clash of views, there follows a great debate (15:7). For a writer of marked irenic tendencies, Luke exposes much conflict in this narrative. Peter's testimony dominates this section. As when he was before the elders in Jerusalem, he prefaces his final question, "Why do you make trial of God?" with the narrative of his experiences. It is, we see, really the narrative of both his and Cornelius' experience, now fully become one story. This is the third telling of the Cornelius episode. It is now reduced to its essentials. The whole sequence is viewed from the ending, and Peter's insight has matured. He no longer elaborates the puzzlement and confusion, but speaks confidently of the story as one told by God. God is the subject of every verb in this account. God chose, testified, did not discriminate, and cleansed the hearts of the Gentiles by faith (15:7-9).

At last, the full meaning of the vision has become clear. Peter was not to discriminate between people (10:20) because God does not discriminate, being "no respecter of persons" (10:34; RSV "shows no partiality"). The clean and unclean of the vision are seen now in this light: "God cleansed their hearts by faith." That in fact God did so cleanse their hearts was certified by the gift of the Holy Spirit to the Gentiles, "just as he did to us" (15:8; cf. 11:15). This is what Peter means by God's witnessing. The question he puts to the opponents is therefore a direct challenge. He had earlier regarded any hesitation to baptize with water those God had given the Spirit as a "preventing" of God (RSV "withstand," 11:17). Now he calls the attempt to impose conditions on the gift of grace to the Gentiles a "testing" of God (RSV "make trial of God," 15:10). Within this tradition, Peter's phrasing suggests an active rebellion against God (cf. LXX Exod. 15:25; 17:2; Ps. 77:46). Peter's interpretative narrative of his experience places the issue on properly theological grounds. Can one recognize God's work in the world? Yes. And once the recognition is made, the church's decision should follow.

Peter reminds his listeners that what he is saying is something they already know. He appeals to their previous experience and understanding: "You know" (Acts 15:7); "Just as he did to us" (15:8); "We believe" (15:11). This last turn is stunning. Peter states as a shared belief the theological truth he has learned from his own experience! The content of this statement is also unexpected. We could anticipate his saying that Gentiles are saved on the same basis as Jews—that would be enough. But his statement actually reverses the situation. He says that Jewish believers will be saved by the grace of the Lord Jesus, *just as the Gentiles* are (15:11). The implication of this reversal is that Peter has come to understand from his experience of God's work among the Gentiles the basis for his own salvation. If those who did not keep the Law were saved by grace, then that must be the basis of his being saved, who had only with difficulty borne the Law. Can it be that Peter and the Jewish Christians needed the conversion of Cornelius more than Cornelius did?

Peter's testimony clears the way for Barnabas and Paul. The assembly listens in silence as they "narrate" all the signs and wonders God has worked through them among the Gentiles (15:12). "Signs and wonders" are the consistent Lucan signal for the way God validates human ministry, from Moses to Paul (cf. Acts 2:19, 22, 43; 5:12; 6:8; 7:36; 14:3). Now Paul and Barnabas, from the perspective of the present, can view the tumultuous and ambiguous events of that journey as God's work, just as Peter could with hindsight speak of his story as one told by God. But just as important, they speak of God doing these things "through them." They recount their own experience of God's activity. The narrative is their only argument. Now it has been joined by Peter's story, so that the narratives of these three missionaries together present a single story for the church's discernment. Although all are apostles, they appear here not as arbiters but as witnesses, speaking in their own voice of God's work in them.

> After they finished speaking, James replied, "Brethren, listen to me. Simeon has related how God first visited the Gentiles, to take out of them a people for his name. And with this the words of the prophets agree, as it is written, 'After this I will return, / and I will rebuild the dwelling of David, which has fallen; / I will rebuild its ruins, / and I will set it up, / that the rest of men may seek the Lord, / and all the Gentiles who are called by my name, / says the Lord, who has made these things known from of old.' Therefore my judgment is that we should not trouble those of the Gentiles who turn to God, but should write to them to abstain from the pollutions of idols and from unchastity and from what is strangled and from blood. For from early generations Moses has had in every city those who preach him, for he is read every sabbath in the synagogues."

We need not ask why James' determination is decisive (for it surely is), but should look at the shape of his decision and his reasons for making it. He makes a solemn judgment (15:19), though one which requires the approval of the assembly (15:22, 25). As the spokesperson of the Jerusalem Church, from which the trouble started, he clearly accepts the basic position of the delegates from Antioch. He considers it wrong to "trouble" the Gentile converts any longer. There is at least an implied acknowledgment that they had been troubled by the Judean party. The fundamental freedom of the Gentile believers (and therefore of God!) is affirmed.

James next deals with the grounds for fellowship. The position of the Christians from the Pharisaic party, that circumcision and the keeping of all of Torah was necessary, is completely rejected. But James thinks that some observances are appropriate. It is important to see why. The first two stipulations—turning away from idolatry and sexual immorality—are axiomatic for Gentile converts as well as Jewish believers (see e.g., 1 Thess. 1:9-10; 4:3-8; 1 Cor. 6:9-11). The biggest concession to Jewish believers is the requirement to abstain from "what is strangled and from blood." Why is this required of Gentiles? This is the sort of regulation that comes into play precisely in the context of eating together, that is, fellowship. And it is intended to enable those who are sincere keepers of the Law to engage in such fellowship with Gentiles. Rather than limit the possibility of fellowship with Gentiles, this requirement opens it, by freeing the conscience of Torah-keeping Christians. James considers these observances reasonable because they would not appear to those who were God-fearers as new obligations at all. So pervasive had been the influence of the Law of Moses in the Diaspora because of the network of synagogues, that even Gentiles would be familiar with these norms (15:21). James decides for the action of God among the Gentiles and resoundingly affirms their freedom and fellowship within the people.

James gives two reasons for his decision: the narrative of Simeon Peter (15:14) and the interpretation of the Scripture (15:15-18). James more than alludes to Peter's story; he makes it his own by adopting Peter's characterizations of the events. He also gives it another level of interpretation. Now the Cornelius episode is seen as the first visitation of God to the Gentiles, and this marks an intervention for salvation (cf. Luke 1:68, 78; 7:16; 19:44; Acts 7:23; LXX Exod. 3:16; 4:31). And by bringing them salvation, God has shaped from among them "a people for his name": The Gentiles are to be regarded as fully part of God's people (cf. Luke 1:17, 68, 77; 2:32; 7:16; 24:19; Acts 3:23; 4:10; 5:12). James recognizes in Peter's story the work of God.

More than that, Peter's story is the key to understanding the Scripture. James' way of introducing the citation is at first puzzling, then illuminating. He does not say, "This agrees with the prophets," but says, "The words of the prophets agree with this," and the reference is to the story

Peter has just told: how God was at work in these events. James then cites Amos 9:11-12 from the Greek translation (LXX), in which the Hebrew, "That they may possess the remnant of Edom," comes out as, "That the rest of men may seek the Lord." James sees that the Gentiles are also "called by my name," and that their conversion means the rebuilding of "the dwelling of David, which has fallen" (15:16). The restored people of God embraces both Gentiles and Jews. What is remarkable, however, is that the text is confirmed by the narrative, not the narrative by the Scripture. As Peter had come to a new understanding of Jesus' words because of the gift of the Spirit, so here the Old Testament is illuminated and interpreted by the narrative of God's activity in the present. On the basis of the narrative and of the Scripture, therefore, James decides for God rather than for precedent.

> Then it seemed good to the apostles and the elders, with the whole church, to choose men from among them and send them to Antioch with Paul and Barnabas. They sent Judas called Barsabbas, and Silas, leading men among the brethren, with the following letter: "The brethren, both the apostles and the elders, to the brethren who are of the Gentiles in Antioch and Syria and Cilicia, greeting. Since we have heard that some persons from us have troubled you with words, unsettling your minds, although we gave them no instructions, it has seemed good to us, having come to one accord, to choose men and send them to you with our beloved Barnabas and Paul, men who have risked their lives for the sake of our Lord Jesus Christ. We have therefore sent Judas and Silas, who themselves will tell you the same things by word of mouth. For it has seemed good to the Holy Spirit and to us to lay upon you no greater burden than these necessary things: that you abstain from what has been sacrificed to idols and from blood and from what is strangled and from unchastity. If you keep yourselves from these, you will do well. Farewell."

The decision articulated by James is approved by the leaders and the whole assembly; they "come to one accord" (15:25). Even the determination of James required discernment and decision by the whole assembly (15:22). The group makes two practical decisions. It will send a letter to Antioch, and with it a personal delegation (15:22-23). Because Paul and Barnabas are highly praised (15:25) and because the Jerusalem delegation is made up of "leading men" who are to confirm the decision (15:22), this letter becomes more than a decree from on high. It becomes an act of fellowship between churches. The gesture is accented by the language of the letter itself. Although the Jerusalem Church denies responsibility for the activity of the troublemakers, it grants that they came "from us," and, by acknowledging that they had unsettled the minds of the believers at Antioch, effectively apologizes for the harm they did. The statement "It has seemed good to the Holy Spirit and to us" is more than rhetoric. The decision reached by the church *has* resulted from the discernment of the Spirit. This church is able to agree with Peter that the Gentiles had received the Holy Spirit "just like us," because it was a church open to the work of that Spirit and able to recognize it in the narrations of others.

> So when they were sent off, they went down to Antioch; and having gathered the congregation together, they delivered the letter. And when they read it, they rejoiced at the exhortation. And Judas and Silas, who were themselves prophets, exhorted the brethren with many words and strengthened them. And after they had spent some time, they were sent off in peace by the brethren to those who had sent them. But Paul and Barnabas remained in Antioch, teaching and preaching the word of the Lord, with many others also.

These decisions have been made by the communities as such. The sending of a delegation from Antioch in the first place was a church decision; so was its reception by the Jerusalem Church. The community, in turn, sent back a delegation with the letter. They are now greeted by this whole congregation. The Jerusalem community fulfills its mission by exhorting and strengthening the brethren in Antioch. They do not simply drop off the letter. The delegates ensure, by their long stay with the church at Antioch (15:33), by their standing in the Jerusalem Church (15:22), and by their being prophets (15:31), that this community is fully recognized as being in communion with the Jerusalem Church. The Jerusalem community shows great pastoral concern for those whom, wittingly or not, it has harmed. It works strenuously to renew fellowship. And as a consequence of these multiple gestures, the Jerusalem delegates are sent back home "in peace" (15:33). So, we understand, there is peace among God's churches.

DECISION MAKING AS A THEOLOGICAL PROCESS

In the story of Cornelius' conversion and the Apostolic Council, we see the early church deciding its future in a fundamental way. It determines how it understands itself as God's people, and how it understands God who calls it as a people. The process is theological. First, it is an articulation of faith seeking understanding, not in some abstract sense, but in an immediate and practical way: How can we understand the actions of God that go beyond our previous grasp of the way God acts?

Second, it is the faith of the church which is articulated. The story begins with the experience of two individuals, and expands step-by-step into a debate and decision of the church as a whole. In the process, the church discovers new dimensions of what "we believe" (15:11). Third, it is the church's faith in God which is articulated. The basic decision, after all, is to let God be God, to say "yes" to the work of the Lord, which goes before the church's ability to understand or even perceive it.

The decision is not made all at once. It is not made by the entire church from the beginning. It is not made on the basis of *a priori* principles and practices. Even the Scripture and the words of Jesus are reread. The decision, rather, is the result of a long process, involving many believers in many places, and the decisions of many local communities. The experiences of diverse people and the narrative of those experiences—in an ever-widening circle—provide the primary theological data. As those who testify speak of their experience of God, so do those who listen weigh what is said: They exercise discernment. The people who have these experiences, moreover, are people already attentive to the Lord in prayer, and thus open to the new and surprising ways God might act, both in their own and in others' lives. Slowly, the story of individuals becomes the narrative of the church.

We see how the stories of Cornelius and Peter interpret each other; how Peter's progressive insight into his vision depends on Cornelius' narrative. We hear Peter telling the tale "in order" before the elders in Jerusalem (11:4), convincing them of the rightness of his decision. We see how the narratives of Peter, Paul, and Barnabas in turn provide the basis for the decision of the church at the Council. The church, in short, is able to discern what God is doing because it is silent and listens to the story of what God is doing in others. Without these narratives, the church cannot discern, and therefore it cannot decide in a theologically responsible way.

In the four earlier accounts of decision making, we saw how narrative and scriptural interpretation were intertwined. In this final account, we have seen two remarkable instances of the same thing. Peter is given new understanding of the words of Jesus because of the new gift of the Holy Spirit. And James reads the prophet Amos with new meaning because of the story of Peter. The words of Jesus and the Scripture are normative for the believers, but in a way that allows new and deeper understanding of them. Throughout these accounts, the experience of God's activity stimulates the church to reread the Scripture and to discover ever new ways in which God maintains continuity with God-self.

Other aspects of the decision-making process in these passages deserve attention: the active role of the assembly and not just leaders; the importance of silence and prayer for discernment to take place; the necessity of opposition and debate openly carried out; the significance of personal and pastoral communication of decisions once made. But I have deliberately concentrated on those components which make the process of reaching decision in the church a theological process: the experience of God, the narrative of that experience, its discernment, and the interpretation of the Word of God.

I emphasize once more that these elements of theological decision making are found in the narrative of Luke-Acts, and only *as* narrative. It is possible, I suggest, to read this text in its literary integrity as a vehicle for theological reflection in the church. As such, it can stand as a witness to the church in every age, asking it to consider whether and in what manner its own processes of decision making are articulations of faith in God.

BIBLIOGRAPHICAL NOTE

For detailed notes on all the passages from Acts considered in this chapter, see L. T. Johnson, *The Acts of the Apostles*, Sacra Pagina 5 (Collegeville: Liturgical Press, 1992). Other treatments of Acts that are sensitive to the ways in which Luke's literary fashioning serves his religious ends include R. C. Tannehill, *The Narrative Unity of Luke-Acts: A Literary Interpretation*, vol. 2: *The Acts of the Apostles* (Minneapolis: Fortress Press, 1990); W. S. Kurz, *Reading Luke-Acts: Dynamics of Biblical Narrative* (Louisville: Westminster/John Knox Press, 1993); W. S. Shepherd, *The Narrative Function of the Holy Spirit as a Character in Acts*, Society of Biblical Literature Dissertation Series 147 (Atlanta: Scholars Press, 1995).

CHAPTER 6

DISCERNMENT

The key element in decision making as a theological process—that is, as an articulation of the church's faith in the Living God—is discernment. It is an essential component at every stage. Discernment enables humans to perceive their characteristically ambiguous experience as revelatory and to articulate such experiences in a narrative of faith. Discernment enables others to hear such narratives as the articulation of faith and as having revelatory significance. Discernment enables communities to listen to such gathering narratives for the word of God that they might express. Discernment enables communities, finally, to decide for God.

But what is discernment? We use the term for that gift of the Holy Spirit for which Paul uses a number of Greek terms. Sometimes he uses cognates of *krinō*, which have the connotation of "judging." Other times he uses cognates of *dokimazō*, which have the connotation of "testing." In 1 Corinthians 12:10, Paul calls discernment of the spirits (*diakrisis tōn pneumatōn*) a specific spiritual gift, and when he speaks of the speech of prophets in the community, he says, "Let two or three prophets speak, and let the others weigh what is said (*diakrinetōsan*)" (1 Cor. 14:29). By "the others," Paul clearly means all the others in the assembly. Discernment is a gift to be exercised by all believers. Likewise in 1 Thessalonians 5:19-20, Paul tells the entire community, "Do not quench the Spirit, do not despise prophesying, but test everything (*dokimazete*)."

From the contexts in which he uses such terms, it appears that Paul regards this capacity of judging, testing, or discerning to be a gift of the Holy Spirit that works in and through human intelligence. Like prophecy itself, it is a gift that uses the mind. We would not go far wrong, then, if we were to regard discernment as similar to the virtue of prudence (*phronēsis*), which the New Testament, like the entire milieu of Hellenistic moral teaching, regards as the capacity to make proper practical decisions (see Rom. 12:3; 15:5; 1 Cor. 13:11; Phil. 2:2-5; 3:15, 19; Col. 3:2; Eph. 1:8). We might, therefore, define discernment as that habit of faith by which we are properly disposed to hear God's Word, and properly disposed to respond to that Word in the practical circumstances of our lives.

THE PROBLEM WITH DISCERNMENT

It is important, if we are to continue together in this conversation, to pay close attention to the objections that many good Christians have to such an explicit focus on discernment, especially as a capacity that can be exercised by everyone in the church. Some point to the way that discernment has been used in practice. Particularly in churches with strong spiritual urges, discernment has been used as a tool for manipulation and mind control. Charges of "false prophecy" have camouflaged personality and power conflicts within communities. Since some are considered to have more "power of discernment" than others, they are in the position to judge whether or not others "have" the Spirit. This is dangerous stuff, and rightly to be avoided. Not even Paul, who soberly declared himself to have "the Spirit of God" (1 Cor. 7:40), presumed to judge the consciences of others, or even decide whether some marriages were "in the Lord," a prerogative later charismatic leaders have not hesitated to assert. The excesses of spiritual totalitarians, so well sketched in Ronald Knox's classic book, *Enthusiasm*, should not, however, make the church abandon this most precious spiritual gift.

Others complain about the church's entrusting itself to something so vague. Dependence on a gift supposedly in the mystical possession of a community appears dangerous, a capitulation to subjectivism. Heeding every so-called narrative of faith could lead to a collapse of standards. A willingness to revise our understanding of our most authoritative texts smacks of fashionable academic post-modernism leading to a moral or doctrinal relativism that threatens our already fragile hold on certainty.

It would be silly to deny that dependence on discernment is dangerous. A more important question, however, might be whether it is not even more dangerous to place our reliance on other norms for making decisions. Is it really the case that we have had better clergy because we have insisted on the credentials provided by professional degrees and psychological testing? What is it, really, that we could lose if we handed ourselves over to the discernment of faith? Would we really lose anything except the illusion of *control*? This question suggests that there may be an idolatrous project underlying resistance to spiritual discernment: the desire for a decision-making process that we can predict and control.

But the obedience of faith offers no certainties, not even that of being certain of our own fidelity. We cannot know if the decisions we make here and now are correct. We only know that they are the best we are able to make, and that in the future we might both regret them and need to change them. The reason has nothing to do with our sinfulness and everything to do with the fact that faith has to do with the Living God, who always moves ahead of us in surprising and sometimes shocking ways. As the Letter to the Hebrews reminds us, business with this power by definition places us in a situation of being in the control of another: "It is a fearful thing to fall into the hands of the living God" (Heb. 10:31).

But is it really the case that relying on discernment means being cast adrift in a sea of subjectivity? Isn't the opposite actually much more the case? Aren't we all so weighted down from centuries of scriptural precedent and ecclesial polity that it takes all our effort to make even a gesture of attentiveness to the stories of others? Our more present danger is that of inertia. All this well-known and beloved story shaped by scripture and tradition, furthermore, provides the context for our hearing of new stories about God's work. Our communities will scarcely reinvent themselves every day. Their choice rather is between growing in response to God's call or conforming to the precedents they have mastered and routinized. Nor should we suppose that decisions made on other bases are more objective. Is reliance on the experience and insight of one or a few leaders less subjective than listening to the experience and insight gathered from many stories? The process of discernment is slow and messy. But it is neither arbitrary nor authoritarian. The same cannot be said for all other methods of decision making.

Another concern: By listening to all stories, does the church place itself in the position of having to say "yes" to every story? This is indeed a subtle objection, because it touches close to the real issue. By allowing or even inviting people to narrate their stories of faith in the assembly, we do offer tacit acceptance if not of the story at least of the storyteller. Must then church become the Oprah Winfrey Show, where child molesters and wife abusers are domesticated by an infinitely tolerant and forgiving audience? I don't think so. The mere existence of Oprah and Donahue and other talk shows and support groups and bonding sessions suggests that the church is not the court of first recourse for compulsive self-revealers. Such folk will derive from the church nothing like the celebrity, dollars, or gratification that is offered by TV, if such is their motivation. If people gather sufficient courage to tell their stories in the assembly of the church, they must have a prior and quite deep commitment to that community and its overall norms. We properly therefore hear them as brothers and sisters, and acknowledge their story as part of the Word God delivers for the discernment of the church.

But why should we define the question in such terms? Why do we assume that these narratives are exercises in exceptionalism, pleas for the lowering of moral standards, or deviations from doctrinal norms? Why don't we assume that they might bring us even more frequently the burden of human suffering which calls for our compassion, or the uplift of human creativity which challenges us to grow? We are called to hear and obey not only by deviance but also by devotion. But in no case does the hearing of such narratives oblige the church to say yes to them. The entire point of hearing the stories of individuals and of groups as they are gathered by shared experiences is to discover how God is acting in the world. But God's work will not be manifested in every story. Some narratives will be not narratives of faith, but of sin and idolatry. To them, the church must say no.

This brings us to the central objection, which requires much closer attention. On what basis does the church say no? How does it distinguish between the work of grace and the work of idolatry, the patterns of faith and those of sin? Does discernment have any criteria with which to work? It is precisely the sense that discernment is lacking in real norms that makes it such a frightening prospect for many Christian communities. It is at this point that it is appropriate to return to Paul's Letters. Paul is the New Testament writer who most explicitly and extensively speaks of discernment, and most emphatically places it at the heart of Christian moral life. I will try to show that Paul's understanding of edification provides the church with a *formal* criterion for discernment, and that his understanding of holiness or sanctification provides the church with a *material* criterion for the task of discernment.

Just as it was necessary for us to remind ourselves of what it meant to read narrative in the case of Luke-Acts, so it is appropriate to clarify our approach to Paul's Letters. Allow me to begin then, with the presuppositions I bring to my reading. I assume, for example, that Paul is not a systematic theologian whose epistles were simply excuses for working out this aspect or that of a grand reinvention of Judaism called Christianity. Nor do I think he was a doctrinal theologian definable in terms of a single truth (like righteousness by faith rather than by works) governing everything he said. All attempts to find the so-called center of Paul's so-called theology fail, because they seek a center of something that's not there. Richard Hays (in *The Faith of Jesus Christ*) is surely nearer the mark when he suggests that what Paul does not explicitly state but everywhere assumes, alludes to, and applies, namely the story of Jesus, governs his thinking far more than any single proposition.

Paul's sensibility, furthermore, is that of the pastor. He is first of all a preacher, sent out by Jesus as *apostolos* to call together churches. He tended and nurtured his communities as a father. In the Hellenistic world, this meant he was responsible for their moral instruction. He would have preferred to "form Christ" among them (Gal. 4:19) by his personal presence, and lacking that, through the delegates he sent "to remind [them] of [his] ways in Christ" (1 Cor. 4:17). Only when those means failed did he write, yet the diversity of purpose and rhetoric in his letters further defies any systematization of his thought. We should look to them, rather, for Paul's primary concern, which was the strengthening of community identity. Paul struggled to think through the connections between the experience of the risen Lord and a consistent pattern of behavior. He tried to help his readers to learn to think in the same way, with what Paul called, provocatively, "the mind of Christ" (1 Cor. 2:16). He meant by this mind a characteristic set of attitudes to be held by all the members of the community.

The proper way to approach Paul's Letters, therefore, is with the recognition that Paul is concerned not with the state of individuals, their holiness, or even their salvation, but rather with the integrity of the *ekklēsia*, God's convocation. This is one of the reasons why both we and Paul's first readers either misunderstand or dislike him. We and they are primarily concerned with ourselves. We, like them, indulge our individualism and elitism, seek some way to measure ourselves against one another, plot our progress toward God by means of greater knowledge, or freedom, or greater physical exertion (asceticism if not circumcision), or more fastidious keeping of rules, or more spectacular varieties of spiritual gifts, or more exalted versions of mysticism. Therefore we now, like them, can be challenged by Paul's call to a larger vision and a concern more capacious than that of our own project. We are invited to edification, the mutal upbuilding of the faith community.

EDIFICATION AS THE TASK OF DISCERNMENT

"Build one another up, just as you are doing" (1 Thess. 5:11). In this earliest extant piece of Christian literature, Paul exhorts the Thessalonians to a certain kind of reciprocal activity, "Build one another up." He also approves the fact that they are already doing it: "just as you are doing." What does Paul mean by the activity designated by the Greek verb *oikodomeō*, which we translate as "build up" or "edify"? Why is he so eager for this to be practiced?

The roots of Paul's language of edification (literally, "building a house") are not entirely clear, nor are they necessarily of the greatest importance. Certainly the social location of the Pauline communities in the household *(oikos)* could have been influential, since the intentional community that was the convocation of God *(ekklēsia)* and the social structure of the household *(oikos)* intersected in interesting ways, so that Paul was capable of referring to the church as "the household of God" *(oikos tou theou,* 1 Tim. 3:15). Undoubtedly, the transfer within Judaism of language concerning the temple as the *oikos tou theou* ("house of God") to a living community of people such as we find in the Qumran writings could also have influenced Paul, and we will find him exploiting just that connection.

An even more intimate (although still speculative) source may have been Paul's own prophetic self-consciousness, for we see him using the language of house-building in the first instance for his apostolic activity of founding and pastoring churches. Thus, twice in 2 Corinthians he speaks of his authority given to him by God "for building up and not for tearing down" (2 Cor. 10:8; 13:10), just as in Galatians 2:18 he had repulsed the thought of turning back to the law as "build[ing] up again those things which I tore down." This language clearly echoes the description of the call of Jeremiah that Paul appropriates to himself also in Galatians 1:15: "When he who had set me apart before I was born, and had called me through his grace" (see Jer. 1:5). The call of Jeremiah continues, "See, I have set you this day over nations and over kingdoms, / to pluck up and to break down, / to destroy and to overthrow, / to build and to plant" (Jer. 1:10). We therefore find Paul using the language of edification for his own apostolic work of founding churches: "making it my ambition to preach the gospel, not where Christ has already been named, lest I build on another man's foundation" (Rom. 15:20). And in an even more explicit double appropriation of the Jeremiah language,

> I planted, Apollos watered, but God gave the growth. . . . We are God's fellow workers; you are God's field, God's building. According to the grace of God given to me, like a skilled master builder I laid a foundation, and another man is building upon it. Let each man take care how he builds upon it. For no other foundation can any one lay than that which is laid, which is Jesus Christ. (1 Cor. 3:6, 9-11)

Paul, it is clear, is working with a complex architectural image. The church is God's house. Its only foundation can be the proclamation of Jesus the Messiah. This is carried out by the apostle, who "lays the foundation." Then others in the community build on this foundation in various ways. Their job is, simply, edification, building up the house of the Lord. The image is found in even more complex form in Ephesians 2:22, where Paul describes the holy temple of the Lord, a "dwelling place of God in the Spirit" which is "built upon the foundation of the apostles and prophets" (2:20). And in Ephesians 4:12, the various spiritual gifts given to apostles, prophets, and evangelists are ". . . for the work of ministry, for building up the body of Christ" (Eph. 4:12).

The questions naturally arise: Who is to carry out this task in the community, and how are they to do it? Paul's answer is twofold for each question. Edification is something that everyone in the community practices, but it is the special province of those Paul terms prophets. Edification involves modes of interaction within the community, but Paul's special attention is on the speech-acts of prophets.

We can move quickly from the general to the particular. Already in Paul's discussion of "God's building" in 1 Corinthians 3:9, he made it clear that he meant his remarks about the complementary roles played by himself and Apollos to function as a model for the community's own behavior: They were not to be in competition, but to cooperate in the work of the Lord (1 Cor. 4:6). He is fighting the attitudes of elitism and arrogance that lead some in that community to consider themselves better than others, since he considers such competitiveness to be destructive of God's building: "Do you not know that you are God's temple and that God's Spirit dwells in you? If any one destroys God's temple, God will destroy him. For God's temple is holy, and that temple you are" (1 Cor. 3:16-17). We will turn explicitly to this idea of holiness later. For now, we note that the opposite of mutual upbuilding is mutual destruction. So Paul wants them to learn from the mutual upbuilding carried out by himself and Apollos a lesson of how they as a community are to act, "that none of you may be puffed up in favor of one against another" (1 Cor. 4:6).

When Paul turns to the specific case of whether they are to eat food that has been offered to idols, he begins with a similar distinction: " 'Knowledge' puffs up, but love builds up" (1 Cor. 8:1). To spell it out: Any knowledge claiming to provide a liberty that can proceed in action heedless of the consequences to others only "puffs up" the individual while running the risk of destroying the community. As Paul puts it forcefully, "By your knowledge this weak man is destroyed, the brother for whom Christ died" (1 Cor. 8:11). How did this happen? Paul plays on his own language: The weak person saw the one with knowledge doing what the weak person thought was forbidden and is "built up ["edified"] into eating food he considers polluted by idolatry" (1 Cor. 8:10). In contrast, the attitude of love is defined by the desire to build up the community in its faith and identity (8:1). At the conclusion of this discussion of involvement with idolatry, Paul again makes the fundamental distinction, " 'All things are lawful,' but not all things are helpful. 'All things are lawful,' but not all things build up," making it as clear as possible: "Let no one seek his own good, but the good of his neighbor" (1 Cor. 10:23-24).

Paul has much the same situation in view when he tells the Roman community, "Let us then pursue what makes for peace and for mutual upbuilding. Do not, for the sake of food, destroy the work of God" (Rom. 14:19-20). And he continues, "We who are strong ought to bear with the failings of the weak, and not to please ourselves; let each of us please [our] neighbor for his good, to edify him" (Rom. 15:1-2). Again, Ephesians draws this together into an image of a growing body, which, "when each part is working properly, makes bodily growth and upbuilds itself in love" (Eph. 4:16).

Paul therefore speaks of edification as that expression of the "mind of Christ" (1 Cor. 2:16) in which each person looks not to his or her own interests but to the interests of others. But he also speaks of it more specifically with regard to *speech* in the community, which draws it directly to our topic of discernment. The directive from 1 Thessalonians 5:11 I cited earlier refers "building each other up" to a type of speech-act, namely, "encouragement" or "exhortation" (*parakalein*). And only a couple of verses later, we find Paul also instructing them, "Do not quench the Spirit, do not despise prophesying, but test everything" (1 Thess. 5:19-21). Similarly, Ephesians 4:29 attaches edification to speech when it instructs, "Let no evil talk come out of your mouths, but only such as is good for edifying, as fits the occasion, that it may impart grace to those who hear."

It is above all in his discussion of the spiritual gifts in 1 Corinthians 12–14, however, that Paul shows the importance of edifying speech in the community. We remember that Paul needs to address the issue of spiritual utterances because of the Corinthian community's fascination with the more spectacular varieties of *charismata*. Indeed, some of them seem to have been claiming that speaking in tongues (*glossolalia*) was the sign of a spiritual person. Paul therefore needs to put *ta pneumatika* ("spiritual realities") in their place.

He begins by making a distinction between "spiritual realities" *(ta pneumatika)*, which can come from any source and lead in any direction— as their experience of mantic prophecy when they were pagans had led them into idolatry—and "spiritual gifts" *(charismata)*, which come from the Holy Spirit. The first way of distinguishing them is in terms of their basic faith commitment. Thus, no one can say, "Cursed be Jesus" when speaking in the Holy Spirit, and no one can say, "Jesus is Lord," except by the Holy Spirit (12:1-3). Then Paul asserts that the spiritual gifts find the basis for their diversity and their unity in the Holy Spirit, who gives to each one "as he wills" (12:11). Of even greater importance here, however, is Paul's statement that each gift is given "for the common good" (12:7); the Greek *pros to sympheron* recalls the earlier distinction Paul had made in 10:23: " 'All things are lawful,' but not all things are helpful *(sympherei)*. 'All things are lawful,' but not all things build up." Clearly, Paul sees the function of these various spiritual gifts to be the building up of the community's identity.

He demonstrates this in three stages. First, he elaborates the image of the church as the Body of Christ: All are equal in this community (Jews or Greeks, slave or free) because all have drunk of the same Holy Spirit; yet that same Spirit has given each member of the body a different function in service of the whole: As in a human body, so in the church, all the parts are interrelated and interdependent (12:12-31). Second, Paul's "hymn of love" in 13:1-13 reminds them of the fundamental attitude of service that must underlie the expression of every spiritual gift, expressed perhaps best in the short phrase, "love does not seek the things of its own" (13:5).

The third stage of Paul's demonstration applies what such loving use of the gifts means in practice, as he distinguishes between the relative merits of *glossolalia* and prophecy (14:1-33). It is here that we find the most useful reflection on the role of discernment in the church. The entire chapter deserves the closest analysis by those interested in our subject, but I can only briefly sketch some of his most important points.

Paul obviously approves of the gift of *glossolalia*. He lists it among the gifts given by the Holy Spirit (12:10), he practices it himself (14:18), and he recognizes this ordered babbling, this linguistic expression of spiritual release, as a legitimate form of prayer (14:2, 28). But Paul insists that its value is restricted to the individual. The person who speaks in tongues builds up or "edifies" himself, "but the other [person] is not edified" (14:4, 17). This is primarily because the ecstatic character of *glossolalia* makes it unintelligible, both to others, and even to the person speaking, since the state of psychological dissociation accompanying such ecstatic speech bypasses the *nous,* or the mind, of the one speaking: The Spirit prays but the mind is unfruitful (14:14). The community cannot say "amen" to statements it does not understand (14:16). Indeed, excessive use of such speech can repel and alienate those who do not possess it: "I shall be a foreigner to the speaker and the speaker a foreigner to me" (14:11).

But there is another problem with *glossolalia.* Such ecstatic and unintelligible utterance is remarkably close to the forms of mantic prophecy current in the Hellenistic world; these "prophets" were "filled with the spirit" and raved. Indeed, this may have been precisely why tongues was attractive to the Corinthians, and regarded as the highest gift, for they were attracted to such patently powerful manifestations of the Spirit. They seem to have sought this form of ecstasy as a "sign of the believer" (14:22). But Paul turns their slogan back on them: In fact, when tongues dominates the assembly, it may become a sign of unbelievers. He pictures outsiders coming upon the scene of an entire assembly speaking in tongues and concluding *hoti mainesthe* (14:23). We often translate this, "you are mad," but it really means, "you are raving as all the other Hellenistic cults rave." In other words, there is nothing special about the Holy Spirit's gifts; they are just more *pneumatika,* psychic fireworks. In contrast, Paul pictures a person coming into the assembly when all are prophesying and being "convicted by all, . . . called to account by all, the secrets of his heart are disclosed; and so, falling on his face, he will worship God and declare that God is really among you" (14:24-25).

Paul's preferred mode of spiritual utterance in the assembly is, therefore, clearly prophecy. Indeed, he will not have people speaking in tongues at all unless they can be interpreted, which means in effect that they are turned into prophecy (14:5, 27-28). Paul wants the tongues interpreted, "so that the church may be edified" (14:5). Paul prefers prophecy because it is a rational form of speech (14:19) that is in the control of the speakers: "The spirits of prophets are subject to prophets" (14:32). But most of all, he prefers it because, being intelligible, it can build up those who hear it: "He who prophesies speaks to people for their upbuilding and encouragement and consolation" (14:3). In contrast to tongues, prophecy is a public gift: It does not speak "mysteries" (14:2), but rather articulates the gospel in a way to transform others, and enable them to perceive that "God is really among you" (14:25). Prophecy is a form of speech that offers itself explicitly to the discernment of the assembly. Paul instructs, "Let two or three prophets speak, and let the others weigh what is said" *(diakrinetōsan)* (14:29); only if they hear in the prophecy the revelation of God's work that convicts and calls the church into account can the community say to it, "amen," that is, "yes" (14:16).

Paul's overall principle for speech-acts in the assembly, therefore, is that they are to be for the building up of the community's identity as the Body of Christ and the household of God. "When you come together, each one has a hymn, a lesson, a revelation, a tongue, or an interpretation. Let all things be done for edification" (14:26). And earlier in the chapter, he made it a still more general principle: "Since you are eager for manifestations of the Spirit, strive to excel in building up the church" (14:12).

In my understanding of decision making as a theological process, I think of what I have called "narratives of faith" in the assembly as roughly equivalent to what Paul calls "prophecy": a form of ordered and controlled speech that reveals God's action in the world and calls the church to response. And I suggest that Paul's analysis of edification as the criterion for the church's discernment begins to give more definite shape to what might otherwise have seemed far too nebulous a concept. Edification is a formal principle that requires material content. But even Paul's discussion of edification itself suggests some preliminary corollaries.

We can state, for example, that the work of discernment has to do with the building of the *community identity* as such, rather than with the praise or condemnation of an *individual's behavior*. Likewise, the activities, attitudes, and narratives of persons evoke the discernment of the community when they impinge on the identity of the community as such. We learn as well that there is a definite connection between the attitudes and actions that "build up" the community, and the speech-acts that "build up" the community. In each case, the criterion is whether the interests of others as well as of the self are served.

Paul assures us that not everything called "spiritual" builds up the community; in fact, it can lead to idolatry. The work of the Holy Spirit is most fundamentally measured by its leading to the confession that Jesus is Lord. A story that does not build on the "only foundation that can be laid, Jesus Messiah" is not a story to which the church should say amen. But Paul goes farther. Not even every action of the Holy Spirit itself actually leads to the building up of the community. The example of *glossolalia* is important, for it shows how a gift might be legitimate but also idiosyncratic, might be valuable and yet not build up the community of faith. And when such private expressions become the norm, the assembly itself might actually become a "sign of unbelievers."

HOLINESS AS THE GOAL OF EDIFICATION

Another passage from our earliest extant Christian writing leads to the next stage of our discussion of discernment: "This is the will of God, your sanctification" (1 Thess. 4:3). Four things are immediately evident in Paul's use of holiness language, beyond the fact—obscured for those dependent on translations—that the terms appearing in English as cognates of "holy" and of "sanctify" are translations of the same Greek terms (*hagiazō, hagiasmos, hagios*). The first is that he uses it with reference to the community as a whole rather than as a quality of individuals. The second is that the language of holiness retains its etymological sense of "apartness" or "otherness." In the biblical tradition, to be holy meant to be different. Calling God "holy" meant that God was, as R. Otto in *The Idea of the Holy* put it, *totaliter aliter*, "totally other," completely off the scale of human measurement. When the Lord tells the people through Moses in Leviticus 19:2, "You shall be holy; for I the LORD your God am holy," it meant that they were to be different within the world as God was different from the world. This same basic sense of holiness as otherness is obvious in the fourth commandment, "Remember the sabbath day, to keep it holy." Torah itself helpfully notes that the sabbath is kept holy by being observed differently: On every other day of the week humans labor; on the sabbath they are to rest. And the reason? So did God rest on the seventh day (Exod. 20:8-11). This leads to the third point: In Judaism and early Christianity, and certainly in Paul, "holiness" denotes realms demarcated by the people's relationship to God. Fourth—and perhaps most startling—Paul does not use holiness language with reference to sacral times or places or things; nor (with one exception) does he use it of ritual or liturgical actions. Instead, he uses it almost exclusively for the identity and the moral activity of the community as such.

Holiness language occurs most frequently in the simple designation *hoi hagioi*, "the saints." It is Paul's usual way of referring to members of the community. The usage may have derived by tradition from the church in Jerusalem, for in three of his letters Paul refers to "the saints," meaning simply the community in Jerusalem (Rom. 15:25, 26, 31; 1 Cor. 16:1; 2 Cor. 8:4; 9:1, 12). Otherwise it designates members of various local communities to whom Paul writes (see e.g., Rom. 16:2; 1 Cor. 16:15; 2 Cor. 1:1; Eph. 1:1; Phil. 1:1; Col. 1:2; 1 Thess. 3:13; 2 Thess. 1:10; 1 Tim. 5:10; 2 Tim. 1:9; Philem. 5). Such regular and indiscriminate use suggests that "the saints or holy ones" is an example of what sociologists call "argot," that is, a group's insider language. For Paul, the term identifies a boundary between those who belong to the messianic community and all those who inhabit that realm designated as "the world" (see e.g.,

1 Cor. 1:27-28; 5:10; Gal. 6:14; Eph. 2:2; Col. 2:20). The assumed contrast between the two realms is illustrated by 1 Corinthians 6:2, where Paul cites as a truism ("do you not know") the fact that "the saints will judge the world." It would be a mistake, therefore, to push each use of the expression to a profounder significance than it can bear. On the other hand, the designation is scarcely arbitrary. It is connected to far more deliberate uses of holiness language pointing to an explicit sense of community identity.

Notice, for example, that Paul can speak of Christians' entry into the community as a rite of sanctification, of "becoming other": After listing the kinds of behavior that are incompatible with the kingdom of God, Paul reminds the Corinthians, ". . . and such were some of you. But you were washed, you were sanctified, you were justified in the name of the Lord Jesus Christ and in the Spirit of our God" (1 Cor. 6:11). Likewise in Ephesians 5:26, Paul says that "Christ loved the church and gave himself up for her, that he might sanctify her, having cleansed her by the washing of water with the word." These passages clearly refer to the ritual of baptism, with a "washing with water" symbolizing entry into the realm of a community ("body") that lived by the Spirit of God: "For by one Spirit we were all baptized into one body—Jews or Greeks, slaves or free—and all were made to drink of one Spirit" (1 Cor. 12:13).

The realm of Christ and the realm of the Spirit are the same, for it is through that "spirit of holiness" given to Jesus by resurrection (Rom. 1:4) that he continues to act powerfully within the church. Paul frequently refers to this Spirit, of course, as "the Holy Spirit" (*to pneuma to hagion;* see e.g., Rom. 5:5; 14:17; 1 Cor. 12:3; 2 Cor. 6:6; 1 Thess. 1:5; 2 Tim. 1:14; Titus 3:5). Both elements of this term are significant. By "Spirit" Paul refers to a power or energy field that is more than material in character, that can touch and affect the spirits of humans in their capacities of freedom expressed by knowing and willing. By "Holy," Paul means that this energy source comes not from any natural or human capacity but from the living God. As Paul tells the Thessalonians, "God chose you from the beginning to be saved, through sanctification by the Spirit and belief in the truth" (2 Thess. 2:13). But since the source of this "Holy Spirit" is the resurrected Lord (" 'the first [human] Adam became a living being'; the last Adam became a life-giving spirit," 1 Cor. 15:45), Paul can as easily speak of Jesus as the source of the Christians' "holiness." The Corinthians have been "sanctified in Christ Jesus" (1 Cor. 1:2), whom God made, Paul says, "our wisdom, our righteousness and sanctification and redemption" (1 Cor. 1:30).

Now it is just at this point that we can observe the remarkable convergence of the two Pauline concepts of edification and holiness. The combination of the notion of the community as a house, and the community as filled with the Holy Spirit, seems inevitably to suggest the image of the people as a living temple. Indeed, the connection had already been made by the Dead Sea sectarians: "When these are in Israel, the council of the community shall be established in truth. It shall be an everlasting plantation, a house of holiness for Aaron . . . shall offer up sweet fragrance. . . . They shall be set apart as holy within the council of the men of the community" (1QS 8:5-13).

When discussing edification, I noted Paul making the same connection. After speaking of the Corinthian congregation as God's planting and God's building (1 Cor. 3:9) in language remarkably similar to the Qumran passage just quoted, Paul continues: "Do you not know that you are God's temple and that God's Spirit dwells in you? If any one destroys God's temple, God will destroy [that one]." There follows the critical conclusion: "For God's temple is holy, and that temple you are" (1 Cor. 3:16-17). Later, of course, when discussing *porneia* ("sexual immorality"), Paul repeats the image: "Do you not know that your body is a temple of the Holy Spirit within you, which you have from God? You are not your own" (1 Cor. 6:19). The English translation might lead us to think that Paul has here shifted to an individual application, but the Greek verbs and pronouns remain plural. Indeed, it is far from certain whether "the body" here refers to the physical body of an individual or the social "body of Christ" of which they are a part. A more literal (Southern) translation of the Greek would be: "Do y'all not know that y'all's body is a temple of the Holy Spirit among y'all?" The presence of the Holy Spirit to the body is in any case clearly a communal concept.

The organic character of the temple image predominates in Ephesians 2:19-22, where Paul declares that the Gentiles, once strangers to God's people, are now "members of the household of God, built upon the foundation of the apostles and prophets, Christ Jesus himself being the cornerstone, in whom the whole structure is joined together and grows into a holy temple in the Lord; in whom you also are built into it for a dwelling place of God in the Spirit." I stress this progressive, growing character of the building-body-temple image, because that leads to the next and critical aspect of Paul's holiness language. The holiness that characterizes the church by the presence of the Holy Spirit is meant to increase by the activities of the members. That edifies the church which builds it up in holiness.

As I turn to this aspect of Paul's language, I want to avoid entering disputed territory concerning the justification, salvation, or sanctification of individuals. Paul's language is remarkably unconcerned with where individuals are on the holiness scale. His language addresses itself to the behavior of the group as such, and to the actions of individuals as they affect the group's identity and integrity. But what is more than clear is his conviction that just as there has been an "already" for them (in that they "have been made holy"), so is there before them a "not yet" (in that they are "called to be holy" [Rom. 1:7; 1 Cor. 1:2]). This is perhaps what is implied by Paul's elliptical phrase in 2 Timothy 1:9, that God had "called them with a holy call," and is certainly implied by Paul's statement to the Thessalonians with which I began this section: "This is the will of God, your sanctification" (1 Thess. 4:3), which is made even more specific a few verses later when Paul declares that God "did not call us to uncleanness but to sanctification" (1 Thess. 4:7). So also the statements that they are to live lives worthy of the holy ones (Eph. 5:3) by being blameless and holy (Eph. 5:27; cf. Eph. 3:12).

The task of sanctifying life in accord with the gift of holiness given by the Spirit is nothing more, really, than a translation into other terms of the Pauline principle stated in Galatians 5:25, "If we live by the Spirit, let us also walk by the Spirit." And it is obvious that the task is not one worked by human effort apart from that power of the Spirit, for as Paul states in 1 Thessalonians 5:23, "May the God of peace himself sanctify you wholly; and may your spirit and soul and body be kept sound and blameless at the coming of our Lord Jesus Christ." So it is God at work in us (cf. Phil. 2:12-13). But there is another aspect of this last passage I want to underscore, and that is the inclusiveness of the process of sanctification: Paul prays that they be sanctified wholly (the term *holotelēs* combines the sense of "completely" and "perfectly"); and he spells this out in terms of ancient psychology: The three parts of the human person (body, soul, and spirit) are to be made holy.

I pause over this point, because it suggests that Paul locates holiness neither exclusively in the realm of the physical body (as a purity system like that of Judaism) nor in the spiritual faculties (as in Gnosticism), but rather in the free human disposition of the self in mental, spiritual, and physical action. Thus Paul refers also in 1 Corinthians 7:34 to being "holy in body and spirit." In Romans 6:19 this is spelled out in terms of obedience to spiritual powers: "Just as you once yielded your members to impurity and to greater and greater iniquity, so now yield your members to righteousness for sanctification." Likewise in 2 Corinthians 7:1, "Let us cleanse ourselves from every defilement of body and spirit, and make holiness perfect in the fear of God."

Paul seldom uses holiness language with reference to specific actions.

The only gesture designated as holy that can in any fashion be considered liturgical is Paul's frequent reference to "the holy kiss," if indeed it was a strictly liturgical action (Rom. 16:16; 1 Cor. 16:20; 2 Cor. 13:12; 1 Thess. 5:26). What is fascinating about the designation of a kiss as "holy" is that the term here clearly plays its role of demarcating boundaries: This is the sort of kiss or greeting we perform within the community (read: "the kiss between holy ones") in contrast to the kisses exchanged by relatives or lovers outside the community.

The only other specific application of holiness language made by Paul concerns family relationships. At least this is the traditional reading of 1 Thessalonians 4:4: "[Let] each one of you know how to take a wife for himself in holiness and honor, not in the passion of lust like heathen who do not know God." While others take *skeuos* ("vessel") as meaning a material possession, the traditional reading (which renders it as "wife") is almost certainly correct, because Paul uses such holiness language again in 1 Corinthians 7 with explicit reference to marriage. In this case, Paul encourages fidelity in marriage even between a believer and unbeliever because of the influence that the believer can have on the unbelieving partner and on their children: "For the unbelieving husband is consecrated ("made holy") through his wife, and the unbelieving wife is consecrated ("made holy") through her husband. Otherwise, your children would be unclean, but as it is they are holy" (7:14). Once more, please notice that in both 1 Thessalonians and 1 Corinthians, Paul's language about marriage within the community of faith stands in contrast to a condition (unclean/lustful) that would obtain outside the community ("like heathen who do not know God"). As with the description of the kiss, holiness language establishes a boundary between inside and outside, between the character of behavior by insiders and outsiders.

I apologize for what must appear in this section to be a barrage of citations, but I wanted to provide you the full range of the textual evidence. The cumulative force of the data, I think, is impressive. It emerges clearly that Paul uses holiness language to describe the character and behavior of the community as a whole, within the understanding of the church as a living temple, the place where the Holy Spirit is present and powerfully active. He uses it, furthermore, not for the cultic actions of the community but for its moral behavior, which is meant progressively to enact that identity (holiness) which distinguishes this group from those outside it in the world.

The evidence, in short, supports just such a connection between edification and holiness as suggested by Romans (12:1-3): "I appeal to you therefore, brethren, by the mercies of God, to present your bodies as a living sacrifice, holy and acceptable to God, which is your spiritual worship [community as temple]. Do not be conformed to this world but be transformed by the renewal of your mind [community sanctification], that you may prove what is the will of God, what is good and acceptable and perfect [community discernment]."

THE HOLINESS OF THE CHURCH

My argument does not yield a set of specific actions automatically identifiable as holy, such as would "build up" the church and therefore challenge the church with a prophetic word demanding decision. But the analysis of Paul's language of holiness does provide us with a powerful heuristic category for further reflection and analysis. It is this: We can regard as building up the church in holiness that which strengthens those elements in the church's identity that make it truly "other" than the world. Conversely: We can regard narratives and prophecies and behavior as destructive of holiness that weaken identity by "conforming to the world."

Specific examples of each sort of behavior appear most obviously in Paul's virtue and vice lists. As Hellenistic philosophers used catalogs to characterize a life lived in opposition to reason, so does Paul use vice lists to identify a way of life that Christians have left behind in their conversion to the true and living God (1 Thess. 1:9-10). Thus, in Romans 1:29-31, Paul lists all the vices of those who, because they did not see fit to acknowledge God, were given up by God to a base mind and improper conduct. Likewise in Titus 3:3, Paul states as contrast to the present state of Christians gifted by the goodness and loving-kindness of God, "We ourselves were once foolish, disobedient, led astray, slaves to various passions and pleasures, passing our days in malice and envy, hated by men and hating one another." The turning is described in most specific detail in a passage cited earlier, 1 Corinthians 6:9-11:

> Do you not know that the unrighteous will not inherit the kingdom of God? Do not be deceived; neither the immoral, nor idolaters, nor adulterers, nor sexual perverts, nor thieves, nor the greedy, nor drunkards, nor revilers, nor robbers will inherit the kingdom of God. And such were some of you. But you were washed, you were sanctified, you were justified in the name of the Lord Jesus Christ and in the Spirit of our God.

Like his contemporaries among Hellenistic moralists, Paul also would have assumed his readers' agreement on the incompatibility of such characteristics with the virtuous life. It was an age certain about basic morality. For Paul, therefore, such patterns of behavior are characteristic only of those outside the community. Thus his outrage that some Corinthians' thought (or acted) otherwise. For Paul, any intrusion of such activities or attitudes within the community threatened the identity of the community as such. Notice in Galatians 5:16-24, how the list of vices is characterized: "I warn you, as I warned you before, that those who do such things shall not inherit the kingdom of God." But Paul needs to use the list to distinguish those within the community who truly live "according to the Spirit" from those who walk "according to the flesh."

The most noteworthy example of the extreme to which Paul himself was willing to go in the case of such behavior was his excommunication of the man in Corinth who was living with his father's wife (1 Cor. 5:1-8). No matter whether this was real or legal incest; for Paul, it was "immorality among you, and of a kind that is not found even among pagans" (5:1). It is striking that as Paul insists on this person being removed "that his spirit may be saved in the day of the Lord Jesus," he makes clear precisely why his behavior was so intolerable: "Do you not know that a little leaven leavens the whole lump?" (5:6). It is the integrity of the community which is at risk: "Cleanse out the old leaven that you may be a new lump, as you really are unleavened. . . . Let us, therefore, celebrate the festival, not with the old leaven, the leaven of malice and evil, but with the unleavened bread of sincerity and truth" (1 Cor. 5:7-8).

How do these observations assist the church's task of discernment as it listens to narratives within the assembly? The vice lists obviously provide a kind of rough-and-ready checklist of those *qualities* in stories to which the church cannot say "yes," just as the virtues provide a checklist of those qualities in stories that are likely to build up the community in its authentic identity. If, on the other hand, we are a generation uncertain as to the very nature of "envy" or "greed," that becomes a different sort of problem. We are perhaps reminded just how much catching up we need to do in our most basic forms of catechesis.

Quite a different sort of difficulty emerges when something identified in the New Testament as a vice comes to be claimed as an essential aspect of a "narrative of faith." One such example, that of homosexuality, will be taken up in the next chapter. At this point it can be said that those who wish to challenge the church to a radical decision that subverts its precedents, must willingly and gladly bear the burden of holiness in their lives. Otherwise, their challenge cannot, and should not, be heard by the church. If such advocates reveal in their narratives of faith the marks of holiness, on the other hand, then their story must be heard respectfully. But as we have seen, there is still another criterion that must be met, not only for these, but for all stories: that of edifying the church. Does this narrative demonstrate a witness to the concerns for others as well as for the self, does it reveal a love that builds up those who are weak?

THE MIND OF CHRIST

Our analysis of edification and holiness needs to push farther. That a life be virtuous rather than filled with vice may be a necessary condition for edification, but it is scarcely a sufficient one. The community that is the church, after all, is not simply a philosophical school. It is a people established by the death and resurrection of Jesus. In the deepest sense, therefore, the boundaries between the saints and the world must be drawn by behavior that corresponds to what Paul calls "the mind of Christ" (1 Cor. 2:16).

This expression comes at the end of the section of 1 Corinthians that began in 1:10 with Paul's rejection of the Corinthians' claiming of one teacher over another ("I am for Paul," "I am for Apollos," "I am for Cephas"). Paul wants the Corinthians to see how inappropriate such party spirit—so typical of the world at large, and indeed of philosophical schools, which always had rivalries between teachers—is for the church. In order to show them its inappropriateness, and in order to set up his later presentation of himself and Apollos as cooperative workers in the "building up" of the community, Paul reminds them first of the conditions of their own calling: It was on the basis not of their status in the world, but just the opposite: "God chose what is foolish in the world to shame the wise, God chose what is weak in the world to shame the strong, God chose what is low and despised in the world, even things that are not, to bring to nothing things that are, so that no human being might boast in the presence of God" (1 Cor. 1:26-29). God's call, in short, reversed the standards of what is smart, powerful, and worthwhile in the world; the church is constituted by such a reversal.

The reason, of course, is the fact that the church is based on the gospel of a crucified Messiah. Thus, Paul precedes his description of the church with his eloquent depiction of the scandal of the cross: The crucified Messiah is a scandal to Jews and foolishness to Greeks (1 Cor. 1:23), because such outsiders seek in Jesus a messiah to meet their expectations that are shaped by the values of this world. Greeks taught by philosophy seek a sage whose strength is shown by impassivity, whereas Jesus shows nothing but compassion. Jews taught by Torah seek a savior whose credentials are proved by righteousness under law, whereas Jesus shows nothing but a life spent associating with sinners and a death cursed by Torah itself. In Jesus, God reversed the expectations of the world as well. But precisely those things which were a stumbling block to outsiders were for insiders "the power of God" (1 Cor. 1:18) and "the wisdom of God" (1 Cor. 1:24), for as Paul concludes, "the foolishness of God is wiser than [humans], and the weakness of God is stronger than [humans]" (1 Cor. 1:25).

When Paul then goes on to describe the "secret and hidden wisdom of God," which is "not a wisdom of this age or of the rulers of this age" (1 Cor. 2:6-7), he does not mean something other than the norm of the crucified Messiah, but means precisely the deeper understanding of the significance of *this same norm*. This is obvious from his most important contrast: "None of the rulers of this age understood this; for if they had, they would not have crucified the Lord of glory" (1 Cor. 2:8). The deeper wisdom for Christians is precisely to comprehend how God has worked in such paradoxical fashion in such clear contrast to the procedures of the world: "Now we have received not the spirit of the world, but the Spirit which is from God, that we might understand the gifts bestowed on us by God. And we impart this in words not taught by human wisdom but taught by the Spirit, interpreting spiritual truths to those who possess the Spirit" (1 Cor. 2:12-13).

By following this passage we have moved from Christology to ecclesiology to discernment without ever moving from the same axis: As the church is constituted by the power of God at work in a crucified Messiah, so must that remain always its fundamental criterion for discerning what makes it uniquely what it is, what distinguishes its "holiness" or "difference" from the world. Paul recognizes that precisely this norm is not recognized by some even belonging to the church: "The unspiritual [person] does not receive the gifts of the Spirit of God, for they are folly to him, and he is not able to understand them because they are spiritually discerned" (1 Cor. 2:14). It is on this basis that he condemns the party spirit and competitiveness of the Corinthians as being, in effect, behavior unworthy of the holiness of the church: "I . . . could not address you as spiritual [people], but as [people] of the flesh, as babes in Christ. . . . You are still of the flesh. For while there is jealousy and strife among you, are you not of the flesh, and behaving like ordinary [people]?" (1 Cor. 3:1-3). The principle of spiritual discernment in the church, then, is the same as the principle of its existence: " 'Who has known the mind of the Lord so as to instruct him?' But we have the mind of Christ" (1 Cor. 2:16).

It is important to emphasize that the passage we have reviewed is not simply one discussion among others in Paul's repertoire of *topoi*. It is, rather, his most extended and fundamental explication of the framework of self-understanding within the Christian community, the essence of what makes it holy, and the basis for discerning what builds up that holiness. His argument here is deeply consonant with that we find in Philippians, where Paul responds to problems of rivalry and envy with the exhortation to "have this mind among yourselves, which is yours in Christ Jesus" (Phil. 2:5), spelling out what he means by that "mind," in terms of Jesus' self-emptying obedience (2:5-11). On precisely this basis, Paul tells the Philippians that true unity in the spirit means looking to one another's interests more than to their own (Phil. 2:4). Paul likewise counters the elitism of the Galatians with the exhortation to "bear one another's burdens, and so fulfil the law of Christ" (Gal. 6:2). He instructs the Roman church to "bear with the failings of the weak, and not to please ourselves; let each of us please his neighbor for his good, to [build him up]. For Christ did not please himself; but, as it is written, 'The reproaches of those who reproached thee fell on me'" (Rom. 15:1-3). And the same principle underlies Paul's instruction to the Colossians, "Forgiving each other; as the Lord has forgiven you, so you also must forgive" (Col. 3:13), and to the Ephesians, "Walk in love, as Christ loved us and gave himself up for us, a fragrant offering and sacrifice to God" (Eph. 5:2).

Throughout the Corinthian correspondence itself, furthermore, Paul rings changes on the basic pattern of reversal that distinguishes the way God has worked in Christ from the way in which the world works, which forms the pattern for the way life should be lived within God's holy temple that is the church. God's wisdom was at work in Jesus' foolishness and weakness, but it is equally so also in Paul's willingness to show foolishness and weakness before the Corinthians (2 Cor. 11:16-21, 30; 12:10; 13:34), and this is to be the pattern of their concern for one another (1 Corinthians 8–10). Christ was rich yet became poor so that the Corinthians might become rich in him (8:9). So Paul has made himself poor for their benefit (1 Cor. 9:15-18), and invites them to dispossess themselves for the sake of the poor in Jerusalem (2 Cor. 8:14-15; 9:6-14). As Christ who knew no sin became sin so that in him they might become the righteousness of God (2 Cor. 5:21), so must they stand not on their own righteousness, but seek that righteousness which is right relationship and reconciliation in the community (5:16-20). As Jesus became life-giving Spirit because he gave up his life for others (1 Cor. 15:45), so are they to bear about in their bodies the death of Christ, so that "death is at work in us, but life in you" (2 Cor. 4:7-12). The holiness of the church is marked by the sign of the cross.

No more dramatic evidence can be given that this distinctive norm for life cuts far deeper than the measure of vice and virtue than the fact that a quality which appeared on pagan philosophical lists as a *vice* became a Christian *virtue*. For philosophers like Epictetus, *tapeinophrosynē*, "lowly-mindedness," was associated with cowardice, cravenness, and lack of nobility. It was a vice because it represented the mind of a slave. Exactly, says Paul, and that is why such *tapeinophrosynē*, the mentality which looks to another's interest rather than one's own, the outlook of a slave, is precisely a mark of the holiness of the church, which lives by "the mind of Christ" (Phil. 2:1-11; see also Rom. 12:16; 2 Cor. 11:7; Eph. 4:2; Col. 3:12).

IMPLICATIONS FOR DISCERNMENT IN THE CHURCH

These observations, I think, open a number of implications for thinking through the specific criteria for discernment in the church. Two seem to me to be of particular importance. The first concerns the manner in which narratives of faith are presented to the assembly. The holiness of the church demands that narratives be presented in lowly-mindedness rather than in arrogance, with a view to the interests of others, not simply to one's own interest, as a means of service rather than as a means of self-assertion. It would follow conversely that those means of "the world" that increasingly characterize our age do not meet the standard of holiness: the shrill denunciation of others, the use of pressure tactics, the techniques of polling and lobbying, the forming of special interest constituencies, even the condoning of violence; can these be taken as marks of holiness that build up the church? Indeed, the entire language of our own age, to the extent it speaks of the "rights" of individuals or groups as absolute and nonnegotiable demands requiring recognition by every assembly, must be recognized as deriving from a spirit of the world and not of God.

A second implication, however, I take with equal or even greater seriousness. The first point might be heard as supporting a passive acceptance of the power groups already in place within the church, and acquiescence in the privileges already enjoyed by some on the basis of tradition and polity. But the principle of holiness itself contains a necessary counterbalance to the quality of lowly-minded service. I mean the principle of egalitarianism in Christ.

Paul's citation of the principle that "in Christ there is neither male nor female, free person or slave, Jew nor Gentile" occurs in the closest conjunction to statements concerning the essential and distinctive character of the church as holy, that is, different from the world. In 1 Corinthians 12:13, it is stated with reference to the one body of Christ: "For by one Spirit we were all baptized into one body—Jews or Greeks, slaves or free—and all were made to drink of one Spirit." In Galatians as well, it appears as an immediate corollary of baptism: "As many of you as were baptized into Christ have put on Christ. There is neither Jew nor Greek, there is neither slave nor free, there is neither male nor female; for you are all one in Christ Jesus" (Gal. 3:28). Likewise in Colossians, Paul connects this principle to the "new humanity" Christians are to assume by their baptism: "You have put off the old nature with its practices and have put on the new nature, which is being renewed in knowledge after the image of its creator. Here there cannot be Greek and Jew, circumcised and uncircumcised, barbarian, Scythian, slave, free [person], but Christ is all, and in all" (Col. 3:9-11).

It has frequently been pointed out—and correctly—that Paul in such statements relativizes the three great kinds of status markers by which humans not only establish differences but also disparities of power between them: race, social status, and gender. It is also clear that Paul considers the church to be a place where such differences are not to count as they do in the world. The differences are not removed, but they are relativized. Their only importance is that they reveal the church as a place of reconciliation: distinctions that in the world always lead to separation, here are perceived as the possibility of gift-giving in peace (see Eph. 2:11-21).

Paul does not consider such egalitarianism as merely ideal. He argues its practical implications in Galatians: An obvious result of Gentiles seeking circumcision as a sign of maturity in righteousness is a church in which only males could be mature Christians. Paul's resistance to circumcision can be read as a statement for the equality of women in the church. Similarly, Paul argues against making either celibacy or marriage a mark of higher status in the kingdom of God by invoking precisely the same principle: "Neither circumcision counts for anything nor uncircumcision, but keeping the commandments of God" (1 Cor. 7:19).

Paul obviously did not himself succeed in translating this understanding of holiness into a consistent norm for the life of the church. When Paul forbade women praying or prophesying without veils, he clearly and explicitly invoked as the reason (when all properly theological arguments failed) the force of social convention and custom (1 Cor. 11:16). When Paul forbade women teaching in the assembly, he relied on a (mis-)understanding of Torah, which conflicted with the principle of equality of male and female in Christ (1 Tim. 2:11-14; see 1 Cor.

14:34-36). When Paul enjoined obedience to the wealthier members of the Corinthian congregation who as householders had financially supported the community (1 Cor. 16:15-18), and when Paul returned the slave Onesimus to his owner, Philemon, despite the fact that both were "brothers in the Lord" (Philem. 8, 12), he himself may well have failed to understand or be obedient to this principle of holiness. And when Paul struggled to place the principle of equality "in the Lord" into the structures of the Hellenistic household, the principle of equality was clearly less evident than the principle of submission (Col. 3:18–4:1; Eph. 5:21–6:9; Titus 2:1-10).

Nevertheless, the surprising thing is not that Paul did not manage this, but that the church in the next two thousand years has not done much if any better. The specific and liberating gift that Paul gives us is precisely both his insight into this deepest demand of holiness in the church, and his imperfect struggle to translate it into the specific social structures of his world.

We can therefore take Paul's lead in asserting that this too is a criterion of holiness by which the church can discern whether a narrative builds up the church: Does it relativize those distinctions between humans which in the world are used to foment fear and hatred, envy and competition, oppression and murder, or does it exacerbate them? Does it lead to a church that celebrates diversity of membership and gift, or one that suppresses and denies that diversity? Does a narrative of faith call the church to genuine impartiality, or does it create privilege and elitism?

The issue of egalitarianism within the church is not a corruption of the church by the ethos of the Enlightenment, but is posed by the church's own truest understanding of the principle of holiness. Outside in the world, background and pedigree and wealth and social status and ambition and power call the tune. In the church, another measure is to apply, one in which gender, social status, and race are not to matter either negatively or positively, one in which lowly-mindedness seeks to serve the interests of others, one in which the temple of God is built up in love. This is indeed a daunting standard. But the subject is not getting along in the world. The subject is building up God's people in holiness.

PART THREE

PRACTICE

CHAPTER 7

DECIDING

The first legitimate use of discernment is in each believer's own search for God's will in the response of faith. Each is responsible for this; no one can assume this responsibility for another (see Rom. 14:4; Matt. 7:3-15). The community as a whole, however, is expected to exercise discernment in matters which affect it as a whole. All are called to discern the words of prophecy spoken in the assembly (1 Cor. 14:29), expel the rebellious deviant (1 Cor. 5:3-5; Matt. 18:15-20), decide matters of leadership (Acts 6:1-6) and fellowship (Acts 10:1–15:35).

The community is neither required nor allowed to judge the salvation of others; that is God's business. But the church must look to its integrity as a witness to God, and therefore exercise discernment concerning the movement of the Spirit within it. But how is the work of the Spirit made available for discernment? I have suggested that what I have called "narratives of faith" can serve as the functional equivalent to what Paul thinks of as prophecy in the assembly. This kind of speech can give voice to the movement of the Spirit within the assembly as a whole, and it can reveal the spiritual attitudes and orientations which motivate behavior within the church. We have seen in the Acts account how multiple individual narratives enabled a community narrative to develop. As that happened, the church was able to exercise discernment concerning the work of the Spirit within it, and decide for God. The narrative of experience is the prerequisite for the kind of discernment required for the church to reach decision as an articulation of faith.

Such narratives are important for all decisions made by the church as community of faith. Decisions on buildings and maintenance may appear banal but can require of a community an examination of itself and its witness. Choosing between new hymnals and a new heating system may test the church's values in a powerfully searching way. The way the members express, by narrative, their experience of God in this church will enable the community to discern which of these choices best articulates its faith. A church which must choose between its aesthetic heritage and the opportunity to make millions of dollars to be used for missionary efforts, if it will allow a skyscraper to be built over its sanctuary, has a splendid chance to articulate its faith in the reaching of that decision, by hearing the narrative of its members' experience of God in that place, and its meaning. Precisely because the situation and story of each church is different, it cannot avoid the responsibility of discernment in such decisions.

Decisions concerning the church's involvement in social and political movements, or issues of public morality, challenge both the community's understanding of itself and the gospel it seeks to proclaim. They force it to ask "What is our faith?" and in the process, they read the Scripture with new urgency, impelled by the narratives of experience of those within the church and those outside it.

HEARING NARRATIVES

By emphasizing the need for the church to heed narratives of faith as though they represented "prophecy in the assembly," it may be thought that I am suggesting that the church's discernment and decision can only go one way, and that is to say "yes" to every such narrative. But I emphatically do *not* think that. Discernment in such an understanding would be meaningless. The church must, if it is to test every spirit, sometimes say "no," for not every spirit is of God (see 1 John 4:1-6). If this is the case for every spirit, it is all the more so with every narrative. Not every story narrated to the church is a story of God's work. Some stories reveal the work of idolatry and sin. For this very reason, it is important that the church hear the narratives. The case of incest in 1 Corinthians 5 showed us a deviance the church could not tolerate and still remain church. The situation of Matthew 18 showed us how an open defiance of the church's authority to correct demanded the rebel's exclusion. We also saw how open opposition in the Acts 15 narrative served the cause of discernment. My point is not that the church can only decide one way, but that the church requires these narratives in order to decide as a community articulating its faith in God.

It is all the more necessary, then, to have some clarity about what should characterize such a "narrative of experience" in the church, if it is to play such a critical role in the discernment process. Both the terms "narrative" and "experience" require some qualification.

I use the word "narrative" for the ordered expression of personal memory. It is not a collection of anecdotes, or a set of opinions, informed or not, on particular subjects. Still less is it the "making of a case," or a kind of polemical pleading. The issue before the church's discernment is not "my rights," but God's will. The decision of the church should be based not on the most powerful pressure or advocacy group, but on the activity of God in the world. This can be offered the church by the ordered expression of personal memory. Because it takes the form of a story, it is available to others more immediately than other forms of speech. Because it is "my story" or "our story," it involves risk and a certain unavoidable vulnerability.

The narrative of experience is a form of witnessing. Like all witnessing, it is personal, but not self-preoccupied or self-referential or self-aggrandizing. One speaks of what one knows, while recognizing that this firsthand knowledge is always partial and interested. Such recital requires sufficient detachment and discipline to order the testimony. The narrative of experience is not a formless exercise in self-expression, but a structured account of personal religious experience.

If the term "narrative" gets at the form of the speech, the term "experience" gets at the subject matter, and it is harder to describe. Clearly, not every kind of "experience" is appropriate for recitation in the assembly. Yet, defining what *is* fitting is difficult. Two extremes can easily be eliminated. On the one hand, the undigested stuff of daily life does not constitute experience for the church's discernment. At the other extreme, peak religious experiences, those encounters with the "Holy" which call us into question, are certainly pertinent, but alone are not enough, precisely to the degree that they tend to stand apart from the flow of daily living.

What is needed is the way such religious experiences and daily life come together, the way what we perceive as all powerful and transcendent gives structure to the rest of our lives: how it actually has given shape to our past and present. The intrusion of power creates patterns in our life. The point of our narrative should be the power. But we need enough of the pattern to locate it.

A narrative expressing such experience is not a form of exhibitionism but a form of praise, showing forth God's revelation in our lives. But here exactly is where discernment is most necessary. The meaning, adequacy, and implications of personal religious experience and history call forth the community's discernment as it seeks to decipher God's Word to it in the present moment. Not every spirit is the Holy Spirit, not every word is God's Word. Not every "turning" is a conversion. Not every kingdom is the kingdom of God. There are "religious experiences" that are not encounters with the true God.

We can, as individuals, and even in small groups of like-minded (or like-experienced) people, mistake the movements of the Spirit. We may be deluded, and, consciously or not, distort both our experience and the narrative of it, shaping them to our desire. We may think we are being moved by the Spirit of God, but may actually be enslaved by idolatry and sin. That is why the narrative is critical, for it includes the results as well as the causes, the patterns as well as the powers, and therefore enables others to discern whether this is the way the Spirit of God works in human lives.

The warning against false prophets in Matthew 7:15-20 twice repeats "You will know them by their fruits," and we can apply this to the patterns created in our lives by the powers by which we live. Paul has listed the fruits of the Holy Spirit's direction: "Love, joy, peace, patience, kindness, goodness, faithfulness, gentleness, self-control" (Gal. 5:22-23). Likewise, he lists the "works of the flesh" which militate against the Spirit: "Fornication, impurity, licentiousness, idolatry, sorcery, enmity, strife, jealousy, anger, selfishness, dissension, party spirit, envy, drunkenness, carousing, and the like" (Gal. 5:19-21). The Spirit of God, when truly at work, leaves traces in our story. The church does have a way to discern the Spirit's work, but only if the fruits are made available by narrative.

I agree that such a process of discernment is obviously hazardous and therefore requires great delicacy. Most of us would prefer norms more steady and machinery less personal for our decision-making process. But the need for spiritual discernment in the process of reaching decision is derived from the very essence of the church's life. When bylaws and customs, or codes and unreflected Scripture citations replace the testing of the Spirit in the church, or, more tragically, when the church proceeds on the assumption that there is no work of the Spirit to *be* tested, then the church may reveal itself in the process of reaching decision, but it won't be as a community of faith in the Spirit.

For the process to work at all, certain qualities are clearly required both of those who speak and of those who hear. On the part of all, a conscious commitment to the presence of the Spirit in the assembly is necessary. Stories should not be spoken before there is the gathering of the people "in the name of Jesus," that is, by prayer that commits this group to the pattern of faith by which it lives. The context in which speaking and listening are done should be one of reverential silence before the mystery, once this commitment to the name of Jesus is genuinely and explicitly made. The community does not seek the display of rhetoric or the flash of personality, but seeks the Word of the Lord. In an atmosphere of silence and awe, there is less temptation to turn narrative into polemic, or discernment into judgment. The community listens and speaks before the gaze of one who "knows the hearts of all" (Acts 1:24).

On the part of those who speak, there should be modesty before the mystery, a simplicity which allows the story to unfold without self-aggrandizement, in either the direction of self-glory or self-castigation. We are not the subject of our discourse. The subject is the work of God in our lives. At the same time, the genuine human texture of experience must be allowed to emerge. The mechanical repetition of platitudes such as "the Lord said to me" is useless. It begs the question, first of all. What the community needs to do is discern whether it *was* the Lord who "said to you," and in what way. The speaker helps the community by letting it see the worldly circumstances of religious experience. This requires of the speaker an attention to real life and how one's response to the Holy has formed patterns of faith and idolatry.

On the part of those who listen, there is as much need for self-discernment and self-criticism as there is for discernment of the other's story. I need to question my presuppositions about God's limits. To be open to new ways of hearing God's Word, I must be critical of the ways my previous hearing has become closed and exclusive. Perhaps God is not speaking to me in the story of the other; but I will never know if I do not allow the possibility that God may be speaking.

The listeners must attend to the story being told and the story already known by the community, testing for what is new and what is familiar. The listeners want to be open to the new, but should be insistent as well on some signs of continuity. If the story rings false, contradicts absolutely the story already told, discernment demands the open and honest expression of objection and opposition. If the voice of opposition is silent, discernment may not have taken place. Tacit approval of every voice, through fear of honest confrontation, will make the church lose its identity as quickly and surely as the rejection of every voice, through fear of change.

DECISIONS REQUIRING DISCERNMENT

It is time to get down to cases. I offer here some thoughts on three kinds of decisions facing churches today. The first deals with leadership and concerns the role of women in the church. The second deals with fellowship and concerns homosexuality in the church. The third deals with stewardship and concerns the church's sharing of possessions. Two of these issues are of a "critical" character, in that they have the capacity to challenge well-established norms. One has a "chronic" character, in that it involves the common and continuing life of every community.

I have chosen these issues to discuss not because they are the only or even the most important questions facing the church today, but for three reasons I hope are appropriate. First, to my mind, they are addressed particularly well by the Scripture passages analyzed in this book. Second, they are issues of sharp relevance to my own tradition as a Roman Catholic, while also of pertinence to other churches. Third, I have personal knowledge of all three issues from my life and my work as a teacher and scholar (thus, I am able to address them at least to some extent from my own "narrative of faith").

Given the argument of the book to this point, I hope it is obvious that this discussion will not pretend to "solve" these issues, or even adequately present them. They are complex and difficult. My interest is in the way that making decisions on these issues might become an articulation of the church's faith, that is, become a theological process. My focus, therefore, is on the components of theology as I have described them, as they can be applied to these situations.

LEADERSHIP: THE ROLE OF WOMEN IN THE CHURCH

To some extent, this is an issue for all churches. Some Protestant denominations have ordained women for years. But the issue of the ordination of women divides portions of the Baptist and Episcopal traditions, and Roman Catholicism remains adamantly opposed to ordaining women to the priesthood. And beneath the specific question of ordained ministry are deeper and more difficult gender issues that are being pressed, issues touching on the roles of women and men generally in culture and in the church, issues touching on the very language used for humans and for God in worship, as well as the adequacy of tradition—and indeed of Scripture—to contain or frame these hard questions.

Because there is such a complex cluster of issues lying just beneath the surface, I deliberately isolate that aspect which appears to me to require the most immediate discernment, and that is women's leadership roles in the church. For communions that already ordain women, the question is what practices and perceptions should follow from that initiative. But for communions that do not yet ordain women, the question is what grounds there are for the decision that has been taken. My exposition focuses, furthermore, on the situation in the Roman Catholic Church. Again, this is my tradition; I am a former monk and priest, while for nine years I have taught women preparing for ministry in Protestant seminaries.

It is striking that within Roman Catholicism, women are seeking to be ordained to the priesthood precisely when, especially in the United States, the ranks of male priests have been alarmingly thinned out by retirement, aging, death, and the dearth of fresh vocations. The signs of a crumbling hierarchical structure are everywhere visible. Catholic seminaries are a fraction of their former number, and have tiny enrollments. Many rural parishes have no priest. Even large urban parishes accustomed to clergy staffs now have one or at the most two priests. The married diaconate fills some gaps but not enough. Nor is the situation likely to get better soon. The recent sexual scandals involving Roman Catholic priests have only further eroded the already diminished moral credibility of the hierarchy from top to bottom, illustrating simultaneously the way damaged persons have been ordained, and the way the institution has been willing to cover up their sins in order to save its own reputation, even at the risk of thousands of children's lives. If there is a single "narrative" that seems to emerge irresistibly from this sad tangle, it is that something is very wrong with the present way of doing things.

The most obvious consequence of the current crisis in vocations is that the sacramental ministry of the Catholic church—and we remember that the sacramental life is the heart of this tradition's identity—is being stretched to its limits. The people are not being fed at the table of the Lord. It may be that God is not leaving the decision in the hands of the church, no matter how many statements the magisterium issues to the effect that only men can be priests, for reasons that are purportedly based in Scripture and theological symbolism, but increasingly seem to be based on fundamental convictions concerning the inadequacy of women. What if an insistence on precedent and prior principle leads to a situation where the sacraments are not celebrated, the word is not preached, the people are not taught, because Christian women have not been empowered to exercise these ministries?

The present situation resembles more than a little that in Acts 6:1-6 (see the discussion, pp. 85-87). In the case of the Jerusalem church also, the needs of the people outstripped the capacity of the appointed ministers. There as well, the current model of ministry was highly symbolic: The Twelve represented Israel, and their table service symbolized their spiritual authority. This understanding, in fact, had the weight of Luke's entire previous narrative behind it. But in the face of the challenge posed by God's activity—the growth in the numbers of believers, the inclusion of new populations, the dissensions caused by the perceiving of inequitable distributions—the apostles were able to distinguish service from symbol. By so doing, they discovered the deeper meaning of their own service and used the symbol to transfer authority to others. These others, we recall, were chosen by the community, which had discerned in them wisdom and the Holy Spirit.

But how can the church today know whether it should reverse two thousand years of precedent and ordain women? It cannot know, unless it undertakes to discern the activity of God in the women of the church today, which can be made available only by the narrative of that activity by the faithful. Such a commitment to discernment requires, as we have seen, the conviction that God *is* active in the lives of all, including the lives of women. The symbolisms of the past will remain intact, and indeed petrified, without the stimulus provided by the work of the Holy Spirit. The Scripture will be heard to say the same thing over and over again eternally, unless our hearing is renewed by the story inscribed among us even now by the finger of God. Without the narrative of the experience of God, discernment cannot begin. And without such discernment, I would argue, decisions are theologically counterfeit.

Whose narratives, then, should be heard in the present circumstances? Those of males who are already ordained, to be sure, including those who have, for a variety of reasons, left the priesthood without relinquishing their loyalty to the church. But the church must also hear the narratives of faith of women in the church. Most obviously, the stories of those now seeking ordination should be elicited and heard. Without a place to narrate the story of what they consider a call from God, how can the authenticity of that call be discerned by the church?

But the church should hear as well the stories of those women who, in their conscience, heard a call from God to ministry, but did not pursue it because of the church's policy. Likewise, and perhaps above all, the church should hear the stories, while it still can, of all those religious women whose lives have been spent in service to the church in a variety of ministries of healing and teaching and administering. This is another cloud of witnesses that, because of the collapse of women's religious orders, is in danger of never being heard. Even if the voice of those women who left religious orders is dismissed because they are regarded as too worldly or disloyal, can the church afford *not* to attend to the voices of these aged and dying confessors of the faith, who pledged themselves to the service of the church and are now spending their last days abandoned, poor, and alone? What might they have to say to the issue of women's leadership in the church? Still other narratives should be heard, including those spoken by members of the church who have been ministered to by women. What testimony do they give? Was the Word of God preached by such women with integrity and power? Were the sacraments celebrated with reverence and care? Was the gift of prophecy and reconciliation alive in them? Was there a distinctive way of articulating the faith available to women, the loss of which impoverishes the church's faith? Did God work "signs and wonders through them"?

Such narratives are available to the Catholic church immediately, if there were the commitment to hearing and discerning them. The churches in which women have been ordained ministers for some time have a narrative of that experience which is available to the Catholic community. But even within the Catholic church, there is a long and powerful story which demands hearing, the story of generations of ministry carried out by religious women, and those ministered to by them. There *are* women in the church who have evangelized, catechized, prophesied, and healed among the people. What is their narrative? And how has that been discerned by the countless Catholics evangelized, catechized, and healed by them? There are also the narratives of women who have exercised leadership in other ways and in other vocations. If these narratives are not being spoken, something is said about the spiritual condition of the church. If there is not even interest in hearing such narratives (because of a conviction there is nothing to hear?), something even stronger is being said.

It is conceivable, if all such narratives were heard and discerned, that the Catholic church's decision to ordain only males would be validated. Perhaps the ministry of women in Protestant communions has been a failure. Perhaps the cost to women themselves is too great. Perhaps Catholic nuns to a woman would insist on their deathbeds that in their view women clergy would be a disaster. Perhaps Protestant women clergy would agree and their communities would as well. It is conceivable, though not likely. What is inconceivable is that a church would not even be interested in hearing what God has done in the world, revelation that is only available through such narratives of faith.

FELLOWSHIP: HOMOSEXUALITY IN THE CHURCH

Homosexuality is an issue that challenges all Christian communities. It does so not only as a matter of moral discernment and pastoral care, but also as a matter of fundamental self-understanding of the church as both inclusive (and thus, in some sense of the term "catholic") and separate (and thus, in some sense of the term, "holy"). Homosexuality poses a hermeneutical challenge to contemporary Christians. The question is not only how we feel or think or act concerning homosexuality, but also how those feelings, thoughts, and actions relate to the canonical texts we take as normative for our lives together.

The case of homosexuality presses on the church's self-understanding with particular severity because on the basis of a certain kind of *experience*, it challenges what appears to be the uniform and unequivocal testimony of the canonical *texts*. I have argued vigorously here that the narratives of experience *must* be heard and discerned, and brought into conversation with the symbols of tradition, if the process of the church's reaching decision is to be an articulation of faith.

Before moving to the specific case of homosexuality, however, it is important to clarify slightly two aspects of the argument I have been pursuing. The first concerns the experience of God in human lives. Nothing could be more offensive than to challenge tradition on the basis of casual or unexamined experience, as though God's revelation were obvious or easy, or reducible to popularity polls. The call to the discernment of human experience is a call not to carelessness, but to its opposite; it is a call to the rigorous asceticism of attentiveness. I repeat: An appeal to some populist claim such as "everyone does it" or "surveys indicate" is theologically meaningless. What counts is whether *God* is up to something in human lives. Discernment of experience in this sense is for the detection of Good News in surprising places, not for the disguising of old sins in novel faces.

Yet it is important to assert that God *does*, on the record, act in surprising and unanticipated ways, and upsets human perceptions of God's scriptural precedents. The most fundamental instance for the very existence of Christianity is the unexpected crucified and raised Messiah, Jesus. A considerable amount of what we call the New Testament derives from the attempt to resolve the cognitive dissonance between the experience of Jesus as the source of God's Holy Spirit, and the text of Torah that disqualified him from that role, since, "cursed be every one who hangs on a tree" (Gal. 3:13; cf. Deut. 21:23).

Another example, as we have seen, is the spread of the gospel to the

Gentiles. Easy for us at this distance, and with little understanding of the importance of the body language of table fellowship, to take for granted such a breaking of precedent that allowed Gentiles to share fully in the life of the Messianic community without being circumcised or practicing observance of Torah. Good for us, also, therefore, to read Acts 10–15 to see just how agonizing and difficult a task it was for that first generation of Christians to allow their perception of God's activity to change their beliefs, and use that new experience as the basis for reinterpreting Scripture.

The second point I want to qualify slightly is the requirement for responsible hermeneutics to take every voice of Scripture seriously. I spoke of the *auctoritates* of the texts as diverse and sometimes contradictory. But every ecclesial decision to live by one rather than another of these voices, to privilege one over another, to suppress one in order to live by another, must be willing to state the grounds of that decision, and demonstrate how the experience of God and the more fundamental principles of "the mind of Christ" and "freedom of the children of God" (principles also rooted in the authority of the text) legitimate the distance between ecclesial decision and a clear statement of Scripture. Do we allow divorce (even if we don't openly call it that) when Jesus forbade it? We must be willing to support our decision by an appeal, not simply to changing circumstances, but to a deeper wisdom given by the Spirit into the meaning of human covenant, and therefore by a better understanding of the saying of Jesus. This is never easy. It is sometimes—as in the case of taking oaths and vows—not even possible. But it is the task of responsible ecclesial hermeneutics.

How does this approach provide a context for thinking about homosexuality? First, it cautions us against trying to suppress the biblical texts which condemn homosexual behavior (Lev. 18:22; Wis. 14:26; Rom. 1:26-27; 1 Cor. 6:9) or to make them say something other than what they say. I think it fair to conclude that early Christianity knew about homosexuality as it was practiced in Greco-Roman culture, shared Judaism's association of it with the "abominations" of idolatry, and regarded it as incompatible with life in the kingdom of God. These *auctoritates* emphatically define homosexuality as a vice, and they cannot simply be dismissed.

Second, however, Scripture itself "authorizes" us to exercise the freedom of the children of God in our interpretation of such passages. We are freed, for example, to evaluate the relative paucity of such condemnations. Compared with the extensive and detailed condemnation of economic oppression at virtually every level of tradition, the off-handed rejection of homosexuality appears instinctive and relatively unreflective. We are freed as well to assess the contexts of the condemnations: the rejection of homosexuality, as of other sexual sins, is connected to the incompatibility of *porneia* with life in the Kingdom. We can further observe that the flat rejection of *porneia* (any form of sexual immorality) is more frequent and general than any of its specific manifestations. We are freed, finally, to consider the grounds on which the texts seem to include homosexuality within *porneia*, namely that it is "against nature," an abomination offensive to God's created order.

Such considerations, in turn, provide an opening for a conversation between our human experience (including our religious experience) and the texts of our tradition. Does our experience now support or challenge the assumption that homosexuality is, simply and without exception, an "offense against nature"? Leviticus and Paul considered homosexuality a vice because they assumed it was a deliberate choice that "suppressed the truth about God." Is that a fair assessment of homosexuality as we have come to understand it? It is, of course, grossly distorting even to talk about "homosexuality" as though one clearly definable thing were meant. But many of us who have gay and lesbian friends and relatives have arrived with them at the opposite conclusion: For many persons the acceptance of their homosexuality *is* an acceptance of creation as it applies to them. It is emphatically *not* a vice that is chosen. If this conclusion is correct, what is the hermeneutical implication?

Another order of question concerns the connection of homosexuality to *porneia*. The church, it is clear, cannot accept *porneia*. But what is the essence of "sexual immorality"? Is the moral quality of sexual behavior defined biologically in terms of the use of certain body parts, or is it defined in terms of personal commitments and attitudes? Is not *porneia* essentially sexual activity that ruptures covenant, just as *castitas* is sexual virtue within or outside marriage because it is sexuality in service to covenant?

If sexual virtue and vice are defined covenantally rather than biologically, then it is possible to place homosexual and heterosexual activity in the same context. Certainly, the church must reject the *porneia* which glorifies sex for its own sake, indulges in promiscuity, destroys the bonds of commitment, and seduces the innocent. Insofar as "gay lifestyle" has these connotations, the church must emphatically and always say no to it. But the church must say no with equal emphasis to the heterosexual, "Playboy-Cosmopolitan" lifestyle. In both cases, also, the church can acknowledge that human sexual activity, while of real and great significance, is not wholly determinative of human existence or worth, and can perhaps begin to ask whether the church's concentration on sexual behavior corresponds proportionally to the emphasis placed on it by Scripture.

The harder question, of course, is whether the church can recognize the possibility of committed and covenantal homosexual love, in the way that it recognizes such sexual or personal love in the sacrament of marriage. This is a harder question because it pertains not simply to moral attitudes or pastoral care, but to the *social* symbolization of the community.

The issue here is analogous to the one facing earliest Christianity after Gentiles started being converted. Granted that they had been given the Holy Spirit, could they be accepted into the people of God just as they were, or must they first "become Jewish" by being circumcised and obeying all the ritual demands of Torah? Remember, please, the stakes: The Gentiles were "by nature" unclean, and were "by practice" polluted by idolatry. We are obsessed by the sexual dimensions of the body. The first-century Mediterranean world was obsessed by the social implications of food and table fellowship. The decision to let the Gentiles in "as is" and to establish a more inclusive form of table fellowship, we should note, came into direct conflict with the accepted interpretation of Torah and what God wanted of humans.

The decision, furthermore, was not easy to reach. Paul's Letter to the Galatians suggests some of the conflict it generated. And as we have seen, Luke devotes five full chapters of Acts (10–15) to the account of how the community caught up with God's intentions, stumbling every step of the way through confusion, doubt, challenge, disagreements, divisions, and debate. Much suffering had to be endured before the implications of Peter's question, "If then God gave the same gift to them as he gave to us when we believed in the Lord Jesus Christ, who was I that I could withstand God" (Acts 11:17), could be fully answered: "We believe that we shall be saved through the grace of the Lord Jesus, just as they will" (Acts 15:11).

The grounds of the church's decision then was the work that God was doing among the Gentiles, bringing them to salvation through faith. On the basis of this experience of God's work, the church made bold to reinterpret Torah, finding there unexpected legitimation for its fidelity to God's surprising ways (Acts 15:15-18). How was that work of God made known to the church? Through the narratives of faith related by Paul and Barnabas and Peter, their personal testimony of how "signs and wonders" had been worked among the Gentiles (Acts 15:4, 6-11, 12-13).

Such witness is what the church now needs from homosexual Christians. Are homosexuality and holiness of life compatible? Is homosexual covenantal love according to "the mind of Christ" an authentic realization of that Christian identity authored by the Holy Spirit, and therefore "authored" as well by the Scripture despite the "authorities" speaking against it? The church can discern this only on the basis of faithful witness. The burden of proof required to overturn scriptural precedents is heavy, but it is a burden that has been borne before. The church should not, cannot, define itself in response to political pressure or popularity polls. But it is called to discern the work of God in human lives and adapt its self-understanding in response to that work of God. Inclusivity must follow from evidence of holiness; are there narratives of homosexual *holiness* to which we must begin to listen?

STEWARDSHIP: THE SHARING
OF POSSESSIONS BY THE CHURCH

In the case of women's ordination and homosexuality, the church is challenged to decision by new experiences that demand a reconsideration of the church's self-understanding of its ministry and of its Scripture. They are by definition situations of crisis. But the church is required to make decision in homelier circumstances all the time. These decisions also involve—or ought to involve—the theological process of the discernment of God's work in the world. Perhaps no decisions are more common, or more in need of theological reflection, than decisions concerning the community's resources.

I have called this section "stewardship," for that seems to be the appropriate term for what is at stake here. Unfortunately, the term "stewardship" itself is in need of rehabilitation. Too often, the term has been used exclusively for the financial support that individual Christians give to their local congregation, or to the appropriate denominational organizations. Stewardship conferences and campaigns are in effect fund-raising ventures. Rhetoric about Christian stewardship is used to stimulate donations to these ventures. In short, stewardship is a mechanism for institutional self-preservation.

Attempts have been made to broaden and deepen the concept of stewardship, not least because the old rhetoric proves less effective in meeting its goals. Thus, stewardship councils have sponsored research that delves into the "biblical concept of stewardship," in the hope of providing a more solid theological grounding for a system of voluntary, institutional financial support. Such research and reflection has worked to connect financial responsibility with a sensitivity to the whole range of possessions the faithful have to share with the community; thus, stewardship campaigns can place financial giving in the context of the stewardship of all ministries within the church, and connect to Paul's language about the apostles as "servants of Christ and stewards of the mysteries of God" (1 Cor. 4:1). The concept of stewardship has also been broadened to include Christian responsibility for "stewardship of the earth," which encompasses a heightened ecological sensibility. When all is said and done, however, that to which "stewardship" continues to refer in ordinary Christian discourse is the financial support of the local church by its members.

More progress would be made if such financial support were simply secularized. The appropriate rhetoric would be: "If you are a member of this community, support its efforts financially." Or impose dues. Or levy taxes. Or, if Scripture must be used, follow Paul's argument in 1 Corinthians 9 that nature, Torah, and the words of Jesus himself all make clear that those who work for the gospel should be supported financially: "You shall not muzzle an ox when it is treading out the grain" (1 Cor. 9:8), and Paul's crisp directive in Galatians 6:6, "Let him who is taught the word share all good things with him who teaches," and the instruction in 1 Timothy 5:17, "Let the elders who rule well be considered worthy of double honor [*timē* = pay], especially those who labor in preaching and teaching." Or do whatever it takes to separate the straightforward and obvious responsibility of any group to its own maintenance from what should be the business of the stewardship of the church, which is its disposition of resources as an articulation and symbol of its faithful response to the Living God.

Such an understanding of stewardship could begin with three convictions markedly lacking from the traditional concept and rhetoric. The first is a *theological* understanding of the role of possessions in the life of faith. What I mean by this is reflection on how the mystery of human "being and having"—a mystery largely impenetrable to us as somatic creatures—intersects the mystery of the human response to God in the conditions of worldly existence. What might be included in this sort of reflection? Attention to the variety and complexity of the ways in which humans "possess": not only their bodies in self-disposition through time and space, not only the obvious "possession" of concrete objects and the financial resources to acquire and maintain them, but also all the mental, emotional, relational, and spiritual "holds" we make on reality to support our claim to *being* on the evidence of our *having*. The reflection would consider as well the multiple ways in which humans are called at every moment to response by the Living God, encountered in all the "others" of our lives. Finally, such reflection would take seriously how the disposition of the whole range of our "possessions" both *is* and *symbolizes* our response to God, mediated through our response to "others" in the worldly circumstances of our existence.

A second conviction that would mark such theological reflection on stewardship is that the witness of Scripture is at least as complex in its witnessing about the human use of possessions, as is our own experience. A serious engagement with this issue would eschew the expectation of a clear and consistent mandate to be followed in all times and in all circumstances. Within the single New Testament composition of Luke-Acts, indeed, there are some six separable "mandates" embedded, ranging from the need to give up all one's possessions to become a disciple, to the need to share all possessions in common.

Serious thinking about the Christian use of possessions in the light of Scripture could begin with the distinction I have made earlier here between "authoring a certain identity," providing "authorities on certain issues," and "authorizing a freedom to interpret." Nowhere are these distinctions more appropriate. In terms of authoring an identity, the Scripture is in fact remarkably uniform: Just as acquiring possessions out of greed and envy is a sign of idolatry and is therefore the implicit rejection of the true God, does faith in the Living God demand the sharing of all our possessions with others. In terms of "authorities," the various mandates of the Scripture must be taken into account when trying to discern what modes of sharing are appropriate in specific circumstances. And the text itself, by combining the clear mandate to share with a confusing variety of *ways* to share, manifestly "authorizes" our freedom to interpret and discern both the witness of Scripture and the ever-changing face of our shared lives.

The final element in a more adequate theological apprehension of stewardship would enlarge its focus from the sharing of possessions by individual Christians in the tangle of their worldly lives, to the disposition of the resources by the *church itself* in the tangle of its worldly existence. The point would be, not how Christians support their institution, but how the church works for the kingdom of God. It is precisely at this point that the concept of stewardship becomes pertinent to the argument of this book, which has concerned itself with the decision making of the church as a theological process involving the discernment of God's work in human narratives. The question for each church therefore becomes: How does our attention to the narratives of experience within our community and outside our community lead us to examine our lives in the light of the scriptural mandates concerning the connection between faith and the disposition of possessions, so that our decisions concerning the use of our resources are in fact a response to the Living God?

The local community is called on to discern such narratives in virtually every aspect of its shared life. Should this congregation purchase new hymnals or improve the day-care facilities for its young families and the workers who use that facility to enable them to hold jobs? The proper decisions are not obvious, but the path to making them righteously is: The community must assess, through the stories of those involved, what the disposition of possessions in each case might mean. And so it is for matters ranging from changes in worship to initiating programs. All involve the commitment of possessions: material, moral, spiritual. All symbolize the disposition of the heart, the response of the community to its perception of God's call.

Sometimes the decisions are agonizing, precisely because they involve choices, not between good and evil, but between one good and another. Should this church use its resources to build a new sanctuary or school building? Or should it invest those funds in programs of care for the needy in the church and in the city? Given such choices, the temptation to simplistic reduction and galvanizing rhetoric is difficult to resist. "Of *course*," one side or another will say, "it is *obvious* what we should do." But of course, it seldom is. The patient discernment of the real needs of the community for worship and education, the real needs of the poor in the community and the city, and the painful decision to move in one way rather than another, demand of the community its best and most faithful self-interpretation. It is not easy to discern between building the ecclesiastical institution and serving the kingdom of God, nor to determine how one might depend on the other.

The point, however, is not that we necessarily decide *rightly*, but that we decide *righteously*. It is beyond our ability as humans always to know the right thing and do it. It is not beyond our capacity to proceed righteously in our deliberations. The procedures sketched in this book are, it must be admitted, arduous and demanding. Nor do they necessarily yield clarity. But if we are convinced that the God who moves ahead of us in all the circumstances of our lives calls us as a community in and through those circumstances to the response of faith, how can we not commit ourselves to this process?

CHAPTER 8

DEVICES

For decision making in the church to become a theological process of the sort I have been describing, there need to be capacities of speaking and hearing within the community. Perhaps the spirit of discernment is alive in a church, but it cannot be exercised for lack of words to tell the story and lack of a framework for the hearing of it. Theology must attend to people's ability to perceive and tell their story as the narrative of faith, as the community's ability to hear it and discern it.

It does no good to criticize present ways of reaching decision unless at least the framework of an alternative is offered. In this chapter, I want to suggest some ways in which the decision-making process might be encouraged in the local church, which has been the focus throughout this book. Because the local church is the best place to think about the *nature* of the church, so it is also the best place to begin to shape a theologically informed way of reaching decision. If such a process is not in place at the local level, it certainly will not be at the ecumenical level. Decisions made at the higher levels of church organizations will remain remote from the church's life, unless those decisions have first been generated by the discernment of local communities.

What I am suggesting here is a way of doing practical theology in a proactive and constructive way. The person who helps the local church learn how to articulate its faith when it goes about making decision is also helping to bring the church into being in the first place, helping the church to become itself. The task is a large one, and the implications are great. Starting to work seriously at this means beginning to move in a direction which has not been heavily traveled for some time. There are not many markers on the path, and the goal itself is still only ill-defined. In this, it is like the response of faith itself, a leap into a larger world whose freedom is immense but whose dimensions and dangers have not yet been wholly surveyed.

A good first step is to recognize the difficulties. Some of these are conceptual and some are tactical. I would like to discuss each briefly. The conceptual problems are the most difficult, because they demand of us something of a conversion of mind, a new way of seeing things. Once we *do* see things in a new light, then the practical difficulties not only appear less forbidding but we have reasons to think it worthwhile to tackle them. Perhaps the chief conceptual problem has to do with the way in which we conceive of ministry in the church. This is a difficulty not only in terms of the "self-understanding" of the minister, but of the perceptions and expectations of the minister held by the people. I begin, then, by taking the most traditional "ministerial" role—that of preaching—and trying to reconceive of it in the terms of this book's argument.

PREACHING AS THE DISCERNMENT OF GOD'S WORD

Preaching in the liturgical assembly is a theological act. Theology in the proper sense is not the study of human opinions but the articulation of faith in the Living God. If faith responds to the living God, then faith is an open-ended enterprise, for the living God always moves ahead of us. If theology articulates faith, then theology also is a matter of constant catching up with the work of the God who acts before we do and most often catches us by surprise. The task of theology is to discern and bring to articulate expression the Word of God embedded, or implicit, within human experience, so that the church can explicitly hear and faithfully respond to that Word.

It is axiomatic for our tradition that God speaks to God's people. So also is the conviction that God's word is powerful and transforming. "The word of God," says the Letter to the Hebrews, "is living and active, sharper than any two-edged sword, piercing to the division of soul and spirit, of joints and marrow, and discerning the thoughts and intentions of the heart. And before him no creature is hidden, but all are open and laid bare to the eyes of him with whom we have to do" (Heb. 4:12-13).

Understood this way, preaching is a high and awesome responsibility. It is not to be equated with teaching, for in teaching the subject matter is outside of oneself and capable of being controlled. In preaching, the subject matter is very much part of the preacher and calls the one who speaks also into question. It is certainly not to be identified with the delivering of bromides, or of nosegays of pleasant thoughts. Preaching is not raconteurship, or the recital of charming anecdotes. It is not even the exposition of Scripture. Preaching is not a matter of providing answers. It is, instead, a matter of both preacher and people being brought into question.

Yet even as we acknowledge that the Word of God "discerns the thoughts and intentions of the heart," we must also confess that the existence and character of that Word in specific circumstances is not altogether clear and conspicuous. That God presses upon us in every circumstance of our lives, calling us to response, we all readily agree. But the precise shape of God's Word is most often obscure, and requires in turn our discernment.

Such discernment of God's Word in the circumstances of human experience is the task of all Christians, but it is given explicit expression by the preacher, just as the response to God's Word in the liturgy of prayer and eucharist gives explicit expression to the inchoate and often incoherent responses of all Christians to the call of God in the circumstances of their lives.

But how can the preacher hear this Word of God in order to discern it and give it expression? The sources are almost too many and too rich, for it is the premise of faith in the living God that God is at work in every circumstance of every person's life. The preacher can discern God's work and word first of all in the preacher's own life experience. Nothing is more repulsive than a sermon that is a preacher's narcissistic "self-reflection." But nothing is more alienated than preaching that has not been worked out in fear and trembling through the preacher's own experience. The preacher has nothing to "tell" others, unless the preacher has first been told; the preacher cannot pose a responsible question to the people unless that question has first been posed by and for the preacher.

Absolutely essential to the preparation for preaching therefore is the prayer of silence. Such prayer is imperative for the life of faith generally—since in it we hear how loud and disruptive our own words are, and allow the silence to still them enough to hear the word God speaks to us through others—and it is critical for the preacher. How else but in silence can the preacher hear the word addressed by God through one's own experience, and where else but in silence can the preacher hear the question put to one's own life by this word, and where else but in silence can the preacher let go of the desire to provide an "answer" for the people and gain the courage to go before them with the "question" posed by God's word?

A second, astoundingly rich, source for discernment of God's Word is the experience of the people. Again the premise: We confess that God is at work, however inarticulately, in the joys and sorrows, the pains and pleasures, the fears and frustrations of everyday life. How else can we discover what God is speaking to us and calling us to, if we close ourselves off from this Word? How can the preacher hope to shape a question that fits experience larger than one's own, if the preacher is not also a listener to such human experience and its discerner? Not only the preacher's own experience but even more the experience of the people must be brought into the process of discernment.

This points to the theological importance of pastoral care and counseling. Pastoral care and visitation is not simply an expression of love and compassion, though it is certainly and most emphatically that. But it is also the opportunity for the preacher to observe and hear in the specific (and often obscure) details of people's lives the ways in which idolatry and grace, sin and faith, are played out. Likewise, pastoral counseling should be thought of not primarily as a therapeutic exercise but as a hermeneutical one: Counseling is the maieusis of revelation, and the counselor is one who can help another hear and discern the Word of God in the thick textures of everyday life.

The preacher, therefore, is one who prepares for the task of preaching first of all by joining in a complex conversation, where the multiple voices of experience diverge and converge. But even as one's own voice joins the conversation, one is listening for another voice, a voice that speaks only indirectly and obliquely through all these other voices. Such "overhearing" is a kind of discernment we all practiced as children, sitting under the table listening to the grown-ups talk, trying to figure out, through all the complex cross-conversation and laughter, what the real topic was. Now, we seek to "overhear" the Word of God that might emerge from all these voices, and which, we are convinced, is the real topic to which we must pay attention and respond.

The preacher also listens with particular care to another set of voices to which the designation "Word of God" has explicitly been attached, the Scripture. It is important to recognize that Scripture is not a single voice, but is itself a complex conversation. It is a conversation, furthermore, that resulted from a process exactly like the one in which the preacher now participates. The New Testament is the literary residue of a set of conversations within earliest Christianity which sought to interpret the powerful actions of God in the crucified and raised Messiah, Jesus, in the light of the symbols of Torah. Torah itself, as we know, is an older set of conversations concerning the work of God in such paradoxical events as the Exodus, the Exile, and the Return. Neither the texts of Torah nor the texts of the New Testament speak with a single voice. In them, also, the "Word of God" must be discerned by careful attention to "the real subject matter" that underlies a bewildering complexity of literary forms, perspectives, and thematic differences.

The constant reading of these texts of the Old and New Testaments is as essential as the prayer of silence and the practice of pastoral visitation for the preacher's practice of discernment as a continuous theological process. Only if the preacher's mind is clothed with these symbols can one's own experience be heard as revelatory of God; only if the preacher "reads" the experience of others with the "mind of Christ" can effective assistance be given to them to also so read and express their experience. Only, in other words, if the preacher is always in conversation with these scriptural conversations will the process of listening and speaking about human experience be one that enables the "Word of God" to be spoken.

The turn to sermon preparation is a matter of making this continuous process more explicit and more focused. Now the preacher intensifies the hearing of the preacher's own experience of the week, month, and year, searching in the light of prayer and the reading of Scripture, for its patterns of idolatry and grace, sin and faith. Now the preacher draws into conversation with the voice of personal experience and reflection all the other voices of the recent weeks, heard in hospital rooms and confessional, spoken in meetings and in passing conversations. And not only the local voices, though these are the most important; the local voices are heard in the context of the voices of the headlines and the issues of the region and nation.

The focus is given by the specific lectionary texts assigned for the day. Using the lectionary is theologically appropriate, for it enables us to respond to the words of Scripture as "other," and prevents us from finding texts that suit the message we want to give. Being forced to deal with texts that come to us from the outside enables us to "listen" to them as we do to other voices in trying to overhear the Word God speaks to the people.

The lectionary also poses some real problems for the preacher. For one thing, although we can *functionally* regard these texts as "other," we know fully well that lectionaries too are the works of human hands. Sometimes, in times of *lectio continua*, the texts from Old and New Testaments come together coincidentally. Other times, we can see the ways in which the selection of the texts has been informed by the desire to make a certain point or reinforce a certain theme. This artificial "closing" of the Scripture, in which a text from the Old Testament is "answered" by a text from the New Testament, requires the preacher's energy and intelligence to reopen, if the texts are to be allowed to pose a question and not a prepackaged answer. The preacher must resist the easy route of proclaiming what the texts obviously invite, for to follow that path would be not to discern the Word, but to manipulate and retail it.

Another difficulty presented by the lectionary is that the texts appear not in their scriptural context but as tiny fragments. For those of us whose only training in Scripture has been through the historical-critical approach, with its emphasis on exegeting passages "in their context," this arrangement leaves us feeling irresponsible. Small wonder that many conscientious preachers think their job has been done when they subject their hearers to an earnest "contextualization" of each passage in turn: "Here is what Paul was trying to tell the Corinthians" . . . "this is what Isaiah's situation was . . ." But the Scripture is read in the assembly not so that we can find out what it meant back then, but so that we can hear how God's word challenges us today.

Preachers need to become more comfortable with the "conversational model" of hermeneutics I have been sketching, and recognize that the fragmentary state of these texts is not unlike the fragmentary patches of conversation heard in pastoral visitations and counseling and reading and prayer. What is needed is to bring these scriptural fragments into play with all those other voices in an even broader conversation.

The preacher might begin by reading the various pieces of the Scripture texts out loud repeatedly. How do they sound in the midst of all the other voices the preacher carries around in the head and heart? It is rare when some sort of connection does not occur, some sort of allusion does not offer itself. Most of all, what is it in any of these texts the preacher does *not* want to hear, or think about, or preach? What is it that the preacher finds offensive? This is the most important clue for interpretation and discernment. The creative preacher can begin from such a point, recognizing that the text is touching on something either the preacher's voice or the voices of the people need to hear in direct proportion to their desire not to hear it.

It is from such a starting point that the preacher can begin to pursue the process of discernment. Was the feeling or sense accurate? Where does it lead, what is the implication? Does the experience of God in this community confirm or question this text? Then what should we do in either case? Does the text challenge the assumption of my voice and the voices I hear among my people of how God is acting because of how God *must* act? Then what should we do about those assumptions?

As these questions are asked, the texts are probed more diligently and vigorously in terms of their original scriptural context. Is the sense of these voices in combination one that can responsibly be attributed to them in their canonical context? If not, do these voices in combination teach us something in the way they converge or collide that none of them could individually?

These questions should move toward a question that truly addresses the experience of the preacher and the people alike. How much better it is for the preacher to provide one legitimate, powerful question out of this struggle with the many voices, than any number of pat or prepackaged answers.

The sermon should be short, and it should be written. It should be written in utterly simple and unpretentious language. It should be written because the discernment of the Word of God is not a matter for carelessness. If the time is short (as it should be) and if the Word has posed a real question for the preacher and the people (as we hope it has), then writing is imperative. Among other things, writing enables the preacher also to *listen* to what is being said.

Is this approach to preaching messy? You bet. Hard to control? Yes. Anxiety-provoking, as the time to speak approaches? Absolutely. All of which is to indicate that something living and real and exciting is happening. Preaching is in danger of becoming a theological act.

LEARNING IN GROUPS TO THINK THEOLOGICALLY

Even when we conceive of our ministry within the church as enabling a conversation centered in the discernment of the Word of God, finding ways of *empowering* that conversation is still not easy. We inevitably come up against the practical problems of procedure. How do we move from one way of doing things to another? The everyday but daunting difficulties of physical bodies and space must be considered here: schedules, room space, lighting, furniture arrangement, and the like. These are not unimportant considerations. It is not easy to practice or learn to practice "discernment of the Spirit" in an auditorium filled with people and wired for sound. A living room or small chapel is better. People sitting in a circle can speak to one another and listen better than if they are all facing a podium. The patient attention to narratives of faith requires some sense of leisure rather than haste and tension. Yet haste and tension, lack of time and space, are what most of us—in families, at work, in our churches—find dominate us.

In light of such realities, it is *imperative* that communities seeking to learn this way of doing things begin small. The first step is forming small groups, and then building slowly to include the congregation as a whole. We confess that where "two or three are gathered" in the name of Jesus, there is a realization of the church. We seek, after all, not a different system of governance, but a new style of interaction within the commu-nity that will foster discernment in decision making. To learn to do this, there must be an atmosphere of trust but also the practical opportunity for active participation. Members must have the time and patience to practice this art.

Learning to think theologically about our lives is not first of all a theoretical enterprise, but a practical one. It is as practical as learning to speak a language. Indeed, it is precisely learning to speak and under-stand a new language, the language of faith. And this requires exercise, repetition, feedback, the confidence that mistakes will not be punished, and that success is achieved by cooperation rather than competition.

Forming such small groups within the congregation, however, will pose at least two other problems. The temptation to constitute groups on the basis of congeniality or like-mindedness must be avoided. Even in its smallest embodiment, the church should be a place where diversity is celebrated rather than suppressed, and differences provide the oppor-tunity for mutual gifting. In addition, when it is time to include a larger portion of the assembly, members of small groups will need to resist the urge to stay within the security of the smaller assembly, where they could speak more freely and be heard more generously.

The biggest practical problem, however, is the perception that there are already too many meetings going on in the local church, more than anyone can possibly attend. Resistance to the formation of still other groups is all too understandable, if they are perceived as "just another meeting." A clear understanding of the nature of such groups and of their importance for the life of the community is important. For this reason, the function of the group must be distinguished from those of other groups already in place.

Not only are there many other meetings, but they tend to systemati-cally separate precisely the elements which need to be brought together, if decision making is to become a theologically responsible process, an articulation of the church's faith. Vestry meetings and their equivalents are the places where the real "decisions" are made in many churches. There, the elected or *ex officio* leaders of the assembly debate and decide the hard issues of finance and personnel; position papers and dossiers and financial reports receive ardent attention. But this business is, well, business. There is little place here for the narrative of experience, or the citation of Scripture, except in the anecdotal and tangential way that makes these meetings long.

Life narratives, in turn, are now told in contexts where decisions—except of the most individual and internal sort—are not made. Personal stories are told in individual or group pastoral counseling sessions, or in support groups—for everything from spousal abuse to alcoholism—sponsored by the church. These narratives, however, rarely focus on the specifically religious dimensions of the narrator's life, and even less frequently are used to interpret the Scripture. Their language is dominantly that of psychology, or self-help literature, or twelve-step programs. These often have a profoundly religious dimension but are not clothed with the symbols of our tradition.

Finally, many churches have meetings for the study of the Bible, whether in Sunday school, adult education classes, or smaller study groups. The emphasis in such groups is usually on the "study" of the text, as guided by contemporary biblical scholarship. This is frequently carried out at a rather sophisticated level, but the element of personal faith narrative is not often found here. And there is even less connection with the making of decisions which affect the life of the whole community.

In effect, then, local congregations often have all the components for theological decision making already in place within the programs and procedures of the church, but they are kept in separate places. This separation narrows and makes less powerful each of the elements. They need to be brought together in a single place and fused into a single process, the catalyst for which is community discernment.

It would be unrealistic and destructive, however, to replace the present structures of the church with a more "spiritual" general assembly in which all these components were joined. There are at least three reasons. First, each kind of meeting has its own legitimate function: There is a place for financial analysis, pastoral counseling, and Bible study in the church. None of these should be abandoned. Second, decisions must continue to be made within the present structure, simply for the community's survival. The world will not go away until we can devise a theologically more sensitive approach to decision making. Third, any move toward a "charismatic" structure would result in chaos unless people were prepared, by having learned to practice (and it is a gift which requires practice) discernment. The church would quickly find itself in the same confusion as the Corinthian congregation. The beginning must be made from below, not from above; it must begin with life, not with order.

The proper beginning, then, is in small groups that gather in the name of Jesus for precisely one purpose: to do theology. The groups must be small enough for face-to-face interaction; large enough to ensure continuance; diverse enough to enable the expression of different viewpoints. The aim is to generate the capacity to think theologically; to detect the experience of God in the context of worldly life; to learn to "narrate" that experience; to discern the movement of the Spirit it reveals; to interpret the Scripture in the light of the manifold narratives of the group; to decide for God. The more this sort of thing is done within the small groups, the more this way of thinking and speaking will characterize the other activities of the church. This is desirable, for it is not the special academic interest of a group which is being cultivated, but the life of the entire church which seeks articulation.

Once such groups begin, however, they face other difficulties more conceptual than tactical. Most people in the church do not know how to tell their story as one of faith experience; do not know how to read the Scripture as pertinent to life; do not even know the meaning of discernment; regard silence as a threatening, not a creative, ambience. In the foregoing section, I sketched how the understanding of the ministry of preaching might begin to empower and model this understanding of the community's life. But the translation of this understanding is extraordinarily difficult. The first task of a group, in fact, might be the candid acknowledgment of these difficulties. They are shared by all of us, for this has not been our way in the church. Few are experts in this process. Those who are have as much to learn as those who are not, for their expertise consists only in this, their desire that the process should begin and the church live as a community of faith. The first story told by us as a group may be the story of how we are incapable of doing this thing we have set ourselves to doing. As each one tells this tale, it moves from the level of a personal inadequacy to a church need. In this way, the moats of fear between us begin to be bridged. This is a beginning. But still greater difficulties remain.

We want to learn to speak of God and God's activity in the world in a way that respects the Mystery, and that also recognizes the complexity of real human life. We wish to develop the capacity to speak God's praises without falling into mechanical and artificial piety. This kind of speech is hard to come by. As different meetings have divided up the segments of the theological decision process, so the linguistic capacities of most believers dwell in separate compartments.

Language that is recognizably "theological" is also, in the minds of many, certifiably dull and mostly unintelligible. Terms like "faith" and "grace" and "sin" have been petrified by generations of pious usage, and are rarely seen to connect to such mundane things as my daily schedule or nightly lovemaking. To ask someone, then, to speak of "an experience of grace" is to ask something literally impossible. The belief about the reality of grace has no correspondence in everyday life but is part of a closed system of symbols. The reality of grace is not easily correlated with the time we fell in love, when I first knew that you knew me utterly as I was and not as I wished to be known and accepted me anyway that way, and how frightening and freeing an experience that was.

The language of Scripture has tended to remain equally inaccessible to life. When I hear Paul speak of "the grace of God," it may leave a warm sensation, but it does not enter the same part of the brain that figures percentages on loans, or analyzes cell structures. And if the words do enter there, I engage in the intellectual game of distancing: "What did Paul mean by grace, anyway?" In either case, I find it hard to connect his words to the depression I feel at not finding work. Not even Bible study, which tells me all I want to know about the Corinthian congregation and the Pauline journeys, helps me see how "the grace of God" has much to do with our sitting in this room together because we are supposed to be thinking theologically.

Another splinter of our language is used to express our life experience. This language is equidistant from that of theology and that of the Bible. When we use the language of "self-revelation," we tend to use a mixture of everyday language and the cliches of sociology and psychology—"psychobabble." We tell our tales facilely as stories of traumas and conflicts, complexes and stages, obsessions and compulsions, self-realizations and self-actualizations. We think this talk simply corresponds to "facts." We are not able or willing to see that this language, too, is conventional and increasingly rigid, and even at best only a formal and partial categorizing of our life. Many of us would not think to tell this same story as one of sin and idolatry, of conversion and faith.

And if there are such watertight compartments in our language, we can be sure that there are also such compartments in our minds and hearts, so that the language about God, the language of the Bible, and the language about ourselves remain sealed off from one another. It comes as a shock when I confidently discourse about my recent nervous breakdown and a friend asks, "Do you think God might be calling you to some sort of conversion in this chaos?" It does not compute. The worlds do not touch.

These separate symbolic worlds can come together, but only by being forced to, and the doing of it is a messy business. That is why groups should have no other task but to learn these capacities. The scholarly study of theology, the academic study of the Bible, and the theoretical analysis of the person will only keep the realms of language separate and increasingly distant. Only in the give-and-take of people committed to the task of learning the language of living faith will the merger be effected.

In the attempt to speak of God with a language which touches ground, and speak of ourselves with a language which reaches beyond ourselves, and to learn of both from the language of the Bible, the element of discernment also comes into play. As I try to describe an experience of transforming power I can attribute only to God, those who listen can ask for clarification, can doubt and wonder, can test my words against their own. And as I, in turn, listen to them, I learn as well to test my story, and discover the deeper resonances of our shared narrative. As children learn the range and nuances of language not alone by hearing but above all by speaking, so do we all with the language of the faith in the church. As grammarians and librarians, theologians and Scripture scholars help us in this our shared task, but they cannot define the language of faith beforehand. Indeed, they need to learn a new task as well: that of listening to as many stories as they can.

The learning of the language of faith, however, need not be altogether haphazard. Two practical steps can be taken to build a living theological vocabulary. Both intend not to coin new words, but to revivify and enrich old ones. The first step is the vigorous use of the insights given by the analysis of religious experience. The religious experiences and convictions of countless peoples, together with their myths and practices, have been carefully described and rigorously analyzed by disciplined observers, whose findings are available in convenient texts. In them, one can find certain consistent components of life before God beneath an astonishing variety of expressions.

One consistent element, for example, is the way religious experiences involve a power which intrudes into everyday life. This power has the ability to organize time and space around itself. Looking at the structure of sacred times and places, therefore, gives us some clues as to the kind of power they point to, and where it appeared. Now, it is possible to shift this kind of observation from those texts to our lives. We can look at the patterns of our lives with new eyes, and wonder about the power which gives them structure. My avoidance of certain places, and my obsessive observance of certain times may have a deeper religious significance than is at first apparent. They may help me see what is truly powerful in my eyes, that by which I measure my worth and around which I structure my days. The categories of religious experience, in other words, can become diagnostic categories for the understanding of our everyday life. This does not happen automatically or even easily, for real life is resistant to such perceptions. Learning to look at life for its significant patterns requires discipline. But it is possible, and it is a beginning.

The language of religious experience is not a panacea, for it can become as abstract as that of classical theology, if separated from the experiences it seeks to describe. But if those using it practice discernment—testing, questioning, supporting one another in the venture—this language can begin to crack the walls between theology and life.

If the awareness of how power draws life around itself helps us detect the patterns of our own existence, it can also help us read the language of the Scripture with new eyes. Why? Because it is precisely to the reality of religious existence which the symbols and stories of the Bible most directly speak. How humans exist before God in the world is the subject of the sacred texts, and they speak as pertinently to our religious experience as to those of our forebears. The stories of the burning bush (Exod. 3:1-6), of the call of Isaiah (Isa. 6:1-13), and of the Gerasene demoniac (Mark 5:1-20) not only grow more vivid when viewed this way, but look increasingly like the stories we tell one another. So the reading of our lives brings the Bible alive, and the reading of the Bible helps us decipher the Word being spoken in our lives. Paul's attack on idolatry in Romans 1:18-32 not only rings true as a description of religious experience, but has frightening power to illuminate and convict our own patterns of clinging and self-deception. The language of religious experience, therefore, can help bridge the now separate worlds of ordinary life, the Bible, and theological concepts. As the two parts of the story of revelation become mutually more reinforcing, less external mediation will be necessary.

Another practical procedure, one already used in many churches, is to begin with the narrative texts of the Scripture themselves as the stimulus and model for the narrative of faith. From the way these narratives speak of God, so can we learn to speak. And as these witnesses never lose the direct touch of the human, so, we hope, will our language about God remain in touch with the contours of our days. Talk about God should not diminish but transfigure the language about God's creation. A group coming together on a regular basis, placing itself in silence, reading a narrative passage together, then allowing its members, one by one, to narrate their diverse appropriations of that passage in their lives, would begin to learn the language of faith.

Many texts are appropriate for this process: The parables of Jesus are used by many people with great effectiveness. Equally powerful are the narratives of the Old Testament, such as those telling of the rise and fall of Saul or the family of David. An almost perfect passage for this purpose is the one which has dominated this particular book, namely Acts 10–15, the story of the conversion of Cornelius and the Apostolic Council. If the story is read section by section, it can evoke precisely the sort of questions which will generate theological reflection.

After coming together in the prayer of silence, for example, let us suppose a member of the group reads of the vision of Cornelius and that of Simon. The first thing that would happen is that the group's perception of itself as a community gathered to hear the words God has commanded would be reinforced (cf. Acts 10:33). The passage then leads naturally to questions about our individual and communal lives. Do we have experiences like these visions? Is our sense of God's presence in prayer as vivid as Cornelius'? Or are we confused and perplexed like Peter? Do we discover that the narrative of others' experiences helps clarify our own, as Peter found in the story of Cornelius a clarification of his own story?

Such questions can be followed by others more challenging, but equally necessary for discernment. How can we say that an experience is from God? How did Peter know, or did he ever know, with certainty? Is it a part of faith that even when you decide for God, you cannot be sure you have? As the story of Acts moves deeper into conflict and decision making, even more provocative questions will be asked of the group, and in the process of answering them, it will discover itself becoming church.

The narrative of Acts 10–15 not only gives us a picture of the church reaching decision as a theological process, but it also gives us a model of what role theology can play in the life of the church. More than that: The narrative of Acts 10–15, when read by the church in faith and discernment, can become the vehicle for doing theology for and in the church. This text can effect that which it describes.

BIBLIOGRAPHICAL NOTE

Among many works in which religious experience is described, certain ones are classic: Rudolf Otto, *The Idea of the Holy*, trans. J. Harvey (New York and London: Oxford University Press, 1958) lacks precision just where one would want it, but the fundamental framework it provides is invaluable. The same can be said of virtually any of Mircea Eliade's many works, of which the most useful might be *The Sacred and the Profane: The Nature of Religion,* trans. W. Trask (New York: Harcourt, Brace and World, 1959). Gerardus van der Leeuw, *Religion in Essence and Manifestation,* 2 vols., trans. J. E. Turner (New York: Harper & Row, Harper Torchbooks, 1963) is drier, but is very fine in its consistent attention to the factor of power in religious experience. Joachim Wach, *The Comparative Study of Religions* (New York: Columbia University Press, 1958) has a splendid first chapter devoted to authentic religious experience. Finally, as an attempt to answer the need for an analysis of Christian religious language that was in contact with real life, so that the discernment of faith might take place, I wrote *Faith's Freedom: A Classic Spirituality for Contemporary Christians* (Minneapolis: Fortress Press, 1990).

LaVergne, TN USA
27 January 2010
171283LV00001B/225/P